James F. Stephen

A Digest of the Law of Criminal Procedure in Indictable Offences

CONTENTS.

PART I.

EXTENT OF THE CRIMINAL LAW WITH REGARD TO PLACE, PERSONS, AND TIME.

CHAPTER I.

LOCAL EXTENT OF THE CRIMINAL LAW.

CHAPTER II.

PERSONS TO WHOM THE CRIMINAL LAW EXTENDS.

CHAPTER III.

TIME WITHIN WHICH CRIMINAL PROCEEDINGS MUST BE INSTITUTED.

PART II.

THE CONSTITUTION OF THE CRIMINAL COURTS.

CHAPTER IV.

THE SUPERIOR CRIMINAL COURTS.

CHAPTER V.

OF JUSTICES OF THE PEACE—THEIR QUALIFICATION AND APPOINTMENT.

CHAPTER VI.

OF COURTS OF QUARTER SESSION.

CHAPTER VII.

OF CORONERS.

CHAPTER VIII.

TERRITORIAL DIVISION OF ENGLAND FOR ADMINIS-TRATION OF CRIMINAL JUSTICE.

CHAPTER IX.

LOCAL JURISDICTION OF THE CRIMINAL COURTS.

CHAPTER X.

LOCAL JURISDICTION IN RESPECT OF CERTAIN SPECIAL OFFENCES, AND OFFENCES COMMITTED UNDER SPECIAL CIRCUMSTANCES.

CHAPTER XI.

OF THE POWER OF THE QUEEN'S BENCH DIVISION OF THE HIGH COURT TO CHANGE PLACE OF TRIAL, AND OF THE WRIT OF CERTIORARI.

PART III.

ARREST, EXAMINATION BEFORE JUSTICES, AND COMMITTAL OF OFFENDERS WITH PROCEEDINGS INCIDENTAL THERETO.

CHAPTER XII.

OF SUMMARY ARREST.

CHAPTER XIII.

PROCEEDINGS BEFORE JUSTICES—INFORMATION—SUMMONS—WARRANT.

CHAPTER XIV.

EXAMINATION BEFORE JUSTICES.

CHAPTER XV.

COMMITMENT WITHOUT PREVIOUS PROCEEDINGS.

CHAPTER XVI.

PROCURING EVIDENCE AT THE EXAMINATION BEFORE JUSTICES.

CHAPTER XVII.

BAIL AND RECOGNIZANCES.

PART IV.

EXTRADITION, FOREIGN OFFENDERS, AND RETURN OF FUGITIVE CRIMINALS FROM BRITISH POSSESSION.

CHAPTER XVIII.

EXTRADITION TO FOREIGN COUNTRIES: GENERAL PRINCIPLES.

CHAPTER XIX.

PROCEDURE FOR ARREST AND SURRENDER OF FOREIGN FUGITIVE CRIMINALS.

CHAPTER XX.

INDIAN AND COLONIAL FUGITIVE OFFENDERS.

PART V.

ACCUSATION.

CHAPTER XXI.

ACCUSATION BY AN INDICTMENT.

CHAPTER XXII.

OF PREFERRING AN INDICTMENT BEFORE A GRAND JURY.

CHAPTER XXIII.

CRIMINAL INFORMATION AND PROCESS THEREON.

CHAPTER XXIV.

ACCUSATION BY A CORONER'S INQUEST.

CHAPTER XXV.

PREPARATIONS FOR INQUEST—JURORS AND WITNESSES.

CHAPTER XXVI.

PROCEEDINGS AT INQUEST.

CHAPTER XXVII.

PROCEEDINGS SUBSEQUENT TO INQUEST.

CHAPTER XXVIII.

OUTLAWRY.

PART VI.

CRIMINAL PLEADING.

CHAPTER XXIX.

INDICTMENTS DEFINED—THEIR DIVISION INTO COUNTS.

CHAPTER XXX.

OF THE CONTENTS OF AN INDICTMENT.

CHAPTER XXXI.

MOTIONS TO QUASH INDICTMENTS—DEMURRERS—PLEAS —MOTIONS IN ARREST OF JUDGMENT.

CHAPTER XXXII.

OF THE PROOF OF INDICTMENTS, AND OF VERDICTS UPON THEM.

PART VII.

ARRAIGNMENT—TRIAL—APPEAL.

CHAPTER XXXIII.

ARRAIGNMENT—PLEA—CHALLENGES OF JURORS.

CHAPTER XXXIV.

TRIAL.

CHAPTER XXXV.

PROCEEDINGS BY WAY OF APPEAL.

PART VIII.

COSTS—REWARDS—RESTITUTION OF PROPERTY.

CHAPTER XXXVI.

COSTS IN CRIMINAL CASES.

CHAPTER XXXVII.

REWARDS, COMPENSATION, AND RESTITUTION OF PROPERTY.

A DIGEST

OF THE

LAW OF CRIMINAL PROCEDURE.

PART I.

[1] EXTENT OF THE CRIMINAL LAW WITH REGARD TO PLACE, PERSONS, AND TIME.

CHAPTER I.—LOCAL EXTENT OF THE CRIMINAL LAW.

CHAPTER II.—PERSONS TO WHOM THE CRIMINAL LAW EXTENDS.

CHAPTER III.—TIME WITHIN WHICH CRIMINAL PROCEEDINGS MUST BE INSTITUTED.

CHAPTER I.

LOCAL EXTENT OF THE CRIMINAL LAW.

ARTICLE 1.

OFFENCES COMMITTED IN ENGLAND.

THE criminal law of England extends to all offences committed

(*a.*) On land in England;

(*b.*) [2] On any landlocked water forming part of the body of any English county.

ARTICLE 2.

OFFENCES COMMITTED ON TERRITORIAL WATERS.

[3] The criminal law of England also extends over the open seas adjacent to the coasts of the United Kingdom and of all

---

[1] See on this subject 2 Hist. Cr. Law, 1–72.

[2] *R.* v. *Cunningham,* Bell C. L. 72; FitzHerbert Corone, 399.

[3] See 40 & 41 Vict. c. 73, preamble and definition of " the territorial waters of her Majesty's dominions." I think the text gives the effect of these provisions. The rest of the text will be found under the article relating to the jurisdiction of the Court of the Admiral (Art. 74).

other parts of her Majesty's dominions, to such a distance as is necessary for the defence and security of such dominions, [that is to say] to the distance of one marine league from the coast measured from low-water mark, and to such further distance (if any) as is deemed by international law to be within the territorial sovereignty of her Majesty.

ARTICLE 3.
OFFENCES COMMITTED ON BRITISH SHIPS.

[1] The criminal law of England extends to all offences committed on British ships either by British subjects or by foreigners, either on the high seas or in foreign harbours or rivers below bridges where great ships go.

ARTICLE 4.
PIRACY BY THE LAW OF NATIONS.

[2] The criminal law of England extends to all acts amounting to piracy by the law of nations committed on the open sea by any person whatever, whether a British subject or not.

ARTICLE 5.
TREASON AND MISPRISION.

[3] The criminal law of England extends to high treason, misprision of treason, and concealment of treason committed out of the realm of England by any subject of her Majesty.

ARTICLE 6.
MURDER AND MANSLAUGHTER.

[4] The criminal law of England extends to the offences of

---

[1] *R.* v. *Anderson,* L. R. 1 C. C. R. 161; *R.* v. *Keyn,* L. R. 2 Ex. Div. 63.   In *R.* v. *Carr & Wilson,* heard before the Court for Crown Cases Reserved, Nov. 25, 1882, it was held that it made no difference whether the ship was under weigh or was moored to the quay of a foreign harbour, and whether the offender was one of the crew, or a passenger, or a foreigner who entered the ship solely in order to commit the offence. It was also held that the flow of the tide and the being below bridges were only tests useful as showing that great ships go to the place of the offence.

[2] *A. G. of Hong-Kong* v. *Kwoh-a-Sing,* L. R. 7 P. C. 179; 2 Hist. Cr. Law, p. 27.

[3] 35 Hen. 8, c. 2.

[4] 24 & 25 Vict. c. 100, s. 9.

murder and manslaughter, and being accessory to murder or manslaughter, when any such offence is committed by any subject of her Majesty on land out of the United Kingdom, whether within the Queen's dominions or not, and whether the person killed were a subject of her Majesty or not.

ARTICLE 7.

OFFENCES IN INDIA.

[1] The criminal law of England extends to all crimes, misdemeanors, and offences committed in India by any [European] subject of her Majesty against any of her Majesty's [2] [European] subjects or any of the inhabitants of India. [3] The word "crimes" in this Article probably includes felonies.

ARTICLE 8.

OFFENCES BY OFFICIALS IN THE COLONIES, ETC.

[4] The criminal law of England extends to every crime, misdemeanor, or offence [[5] not amounting to felony] committed by any person employed by or in the service of her Majesty in any civil or military station, office, capacity, or employment out of Great Britain in the execution or under colour or in the exercise of any such station, office, capacity, or employment.

ARTICLE 9.

OPPRESSION BY COLONIAL GOVERNORS.

[6] The criminal law of England extends to governors, lieutenant-governors, deputy-governors, and commanders-in-chief of all plantations and colonies within her Majesty's dominions beyond the seas who are guilty of oppressing any of her Majesty's subjects beyond the seas within their respective

---

[1] 13 Geo. 3, c. 63, s. 39.

[2] This is obviously the meaning of the Act. The Governor-General and other principal officials in India are expressly named.

[3] See proviso in s. 45, implying that "capital cases" may be tried under the Act.

[4] 42 Geo. 3, c. 85, s. 1.

[5] *R.* v. *Shawe,* 5 M. & S. 403.

[6] 11 & 12 Will. 3, c. 12.

governments or commands, or of any other [1] crime or offence
contrary to the laws of this realm, or in force within their
respective governments or commands.

ARTICLE 10.

INCITING TO MUTINY.

[2] The Act relating to the offence of inciting troops to
mutiny [3] seems to apply to all places in which her Majesty's
forces may be serving by sea or land.

ARTICLE 11.

FOREIGN ENLISTMENT ACT.

[4] The Foreign Enlistment Act, 1870, s. 4, applies to every
British subject within or without her Majesty's dominions.

The other sections of the said Act which create offences
apply to all the dominions of her Majesty, including the
adjacent territorial waters.

ARTICLE 12.

SLAVE TRADE.

[5] The Slave Trade Act, 1824, s. 9, extends to all subjects
of her Majesty, and to all persons residing or being within
any of her Majesty's dominions, including India or any
dominion, fort, settlement, factory, or territory in her
Majesty's occupation or possession, who, upon the high seas
or in any haven, river, creek, or place where the admiral has
jurisdiction, does any of the things · forbidden by that
enactment.

---

[1] There is nothing to show whether this includes felonies or not, except that
the general scope of the Act seems to be confined to misdemeanors.

[2] 37 Geo. 3, c. 70.

[3] The words of the Act are "endeavour to seduce any person serving in his
Majesty's forces by sea or land"; and s. 2 provides for the place of prosecution
when the crime is committed either on the high seas or in England. It is
silent as to the commission of the offence on land abroad. Hence I have expressed
myself doubtfully.

[4] 33 & 34 Vict. c. 90, s. 4.

[5] 5 Geo. 4, c. 114, s. 9.

¹ The 10th section of the same Act seems to apply to all acts done in any part of the world by any person in any of her Majesty's dominions, or by any British subject, whether in or out of her Majesty's dominions.

ARTICLE 13.

BIGAMY.

² The 57th section of the Offences against the Person Act, 1861 (relating to bigamy), extends to marriages contracted by her Majesty's subjects in any part of the world, and to marriages contracted in England or Ireland by any person already validly married in any part of the world.

The word "marriage" in this article does not include connections avowedly polygamous.

---

¹ *R.* v. *Zulueta*, 1 C. & K. 215; and see *Santos* v. *Illidge*, 8 C. B. (N.S.) 861. A, a foreigner in England who buys and sells slaves in Brazil, and B, an Englishman in Brazil who buys and sells slaves in Brazil, both appear to be within the section, but the case of B has never been decided definitely.

² 24 & 25 Vict. c. 100, s. 57; and see Digest, p. 174, Article 257

CHAPTER II.

PERSONS TO WHOM THE CRIMINAL LAW EXTENDS.

ARTICLE 14.

PERSONS TO WHOM THE CRIMINAL LAW EXTENDS.

[1] THE criminal law extends to all persons whatever, except her Majesty the Queen, who is absolutely exempt from it, and foreign ambassadors, who are probably exempt from it to an extent which has never been precisely determined.

It is doubtful how far it extends to prisoners of war brought into and detained in England against their will, and it probably does not extend to acts done by persons subject to the discipline of foreign ships of war in British harbours or other waters, so long as such acts affect such persons only, and if such persons are not British subjects.

[1] 2 Hist. Cr. Law, 2–9 and 43–56.

CHAPTER III.

TIME WITHIN WHICH CRIMINAL PROCEEDINGS MUST BE INSTITUTED.

ARTICLE 15.

[1] TIME WITHIN WHICH CRIMINAL PROCEEDINGS MUST BE INSTITUTED.

CRIMINAL proceedings may be instituted at any time during the life of the person charged, except in the following cases :—

[2] In cases of treason (other than designing, endeavouring, or attempting any assassination on the body of her Majesty by poison or otherwise) and in cases of misprision of treason committed in England, Wales, or Berwick-on-Tweed, the indictment must be found by the grand jury within three years next after the treason or offence done and committed.

[3] No person can be prosecuted for any offence against 1 Geo. 1, st. 2, c. 5, unless the prosecution is commenced within twelve months after the offence committed.

No person can be prosecuted by virtue of [4] 9 Will. 3, c. 35, for any words spoken unless information of such words is given upon oath before a justice within four days after they are spoken, and the prosecution of the offence is within three months of such information.

[5] No one can be prosecuted for any offence against 60 Geo.

---

[1] 2 Hist. Cr. Law, 1–2.

[2] 7 & 8 Will. 3, c. 3, ss. 5 & 6. The actual assassination of the sovereign is not included in the exception. The section is said by Foster (p. 249) to apply to Scotland; it does not apply to Ireland, or to treason committed abroad.

[3] 1 Geo. 1, st. 2, c. 5, s. 8. This is the Riot Act ; see Digest, Article 73.

[4] 9 Will. 3, c. 35, s. 2. Punishing blasphemy, &c. Digest, Article 163.

[5] 60 Geo. 3 & 1 Geo. 4, c. 1, s. 7. An Act against illegal drilling. See Digest, Article 82.

3 & 1 Geo. 4, c. 1, unless such prosecution is commenced within six calendar months after the offence committed.

[1] The prosecution for every offence punishable upon indictment or otherwise than upon summary conviction under 9 Geo. 4, c. 69, must be commenced within six months after the offence.

[2] In cases in which no time is specially limited for making a complaint or information as hereinafter mentioned in respect of an offence punishable on summary conviction otherwise than under 18 & 19 Vict. c. 126, the complaint must be made or the information laid within six months from the time when the matter thereof arose.

[3] Offences committed in India by official persons employed there must, if prosecuted in England, be prosecuted within six years after the offence committed. [4] If prosecuted before the Special Parliamentary Court constituted by 24 Geo. 3, Sess. 2, c. 25, they must be prosecuted within three years after the offender leaves India.

[1] 9 Geo. 4, c. 69, s. 4. Offences relating to game. See Digest, Articles 77, 385. The information, if there is one, appears to be the "commencement of the prosecution." *R. v. Parker*, L. & C. 459.

[2] 11 & 12 Vict. c. 43, s. 11. Does this apply to summary convictions for felony?

[3] 33 Geo. 3, c. 52, s. 140.

[4] 24 Geo. 3, Sess. 2, c. 25, s. 82.

PART II.

[1]THE CONSTITUTION OF THE CRIMINAL COURTS.

CHAPTER IV.

THE SUPERIOR CRIMINAL COURTS.

Article 16.

ENUMERATION OF THE SUPERIOR CRIMINAL COURTS.

There are in England the following superior Courts of a criminal jurisdiction :—

[2] The House of Lords.

[3] The Court of the Lord High Steward.

[4] The High Court of Justice (Queen's Bench Division).

---

[1] 1 Hist. Cr. Law, ch. iv. v. vi. pp. 75–183.

[2] 1 Hist. Cr. Law, 145.

[3] 1 Hist. Cr. Law, 164.

[4] 1 Hist. Cr. Law, 85.

[1] The Courts of the Commissioners of Assize, Oyer and Terminer, and Gaol Delivery.

[2] The Central Criminal Court.

[3] The Court of the Lord High Admiral of England.

ARTICLE 17.
THE HOUSE OF LORDS.

[4] The House of Lords is a Court of Justice of which all the Peers of Parliament, including the Bishops, are Judges (though the Bishops are excused from voting in capital cases), and of which the Lord High Steward, [5] if a Lord High Steward is appointed for that purpose by her Majesty, is the President. The Lords who take part in the proceedings are judges both of the law and of the fact.

ARTICLE 18.
THE COURT OF THE LORD HIGH STEWARD.

[6] The Court of the Lord High Steward is a Court which may be convened when Parliament is not sitting. It consists of the Lord High Steward and as many Peers of Parliament as are summoned and appear. The Lord High Steward is judge of the law, and the other Lords, who are called Lords Triers, are judges of the facts.

ARTICLE 19.
TRIALS FOR TREASON AND MISPRISION IN THE HOUSE OF LORDS AND THE COURT OF THE LORD HIGH STEWARD.

[7] Whenever any person is to be tried for high treason or for misprision of treason, either by the House of Lords or in the Court of the Lord High Steward, all the Peers who have a right to sit and vote in Parliament must be summoned,

---

[1] 1 Hist. Cr. Law, 97.
[2] 1 Hist. Cr. Law, 118.
[3] 2 Hist. Cr. Law, 16–26.
[4] 4 Ste. Com. 296; 2 Hawk. 580. 1 Hist. Cr. Law. ch. v. p. 145.
[5] This is always done in practice.
[6] 2 Hawk. 580, &c. 1 Hist. Cr. Law. ch. v.
[7] 7 & 8 Will. 3, c. 3, s. 10.

twenty days at least before the trial, and every Peer so summoned and appearing at the trial must vote.

It is not certain how many Peers ought to be summoned to sit as Lords Triers if the trial is to be for any offence other than treason or misprision of treason.

The Lord High Steward is appointed by Commission from the Crown for each occasion on which his services are required.

ARTICLE 20.

EXCLUSIVE JURISDICTION OF HOUSE OF LORDS IN RESPECT OF PERSONS AND OFFENCES.

[1] The House of Lords has during the Session of Parliament exclusive jurisdiction over all Lords of Parliament, including such Bishops as are such Lords, and Peeresses in their own right or in the right of their husbands, and over all Scotch and Irish Peers and Peeresses in their own right or in the right of their husbands, in cases of treason and misprision of treason and felony, whether upon impeachment or upon an indictment.

[2] When Parliament is not sitting the Court of the Lord High Steward has the same jurisdiction over the same persons (except Bishops being Lords of Parliament), for the same offences upon an indictment therefor.

ARTICLE 21.

JURISDICTION OF HOUSE OF LORDS ON IMPEACHMENT BY THE HOUSE OF COMMONS.

[3] The House of Lords has jurisdiction over all persons impeached by the House of Commons for any misdemeanor.

ARTICLE 22.

THE HIGH COURT OF JUSTICE (QUEEN'S BENCH DIVISION).

The High Court of Justice (Queen's Bench Division) is

---

[1] 2 Hawk. P. C. 580–5. As to Bishops, see p. 584; as to Peeresses by marriage, 20 Hen. 6; for an instance of such a trial see *Duchess of Kingston's Case*, 20 St. Tr. 385. As to Scotch Peers, 6 Anne, c. 11, Article 23. As to Irish Peers, 39 & 40 Geo. 3, c. 67, Article 4. 1 Hist. Cr. Law, 161–6.

[2] 4 Ste. Com. 296.

[3] 4 Ste. Com. 293. 1 Hist. Cr. Law, ch. v. p. 146.

constituted by the Supreme Court of Judicature Act, 36 & 37 Vict. c. 66, and [1] consists of the Lord Chief Justice of England, who is President thereof, and such other Judges as are members of the said division.

ARTICLE 23.

[2] THE CROWN COURTS AT THE ASSIZES.

The Crown Courts at the Assizes are Courts held by one or more Commissioners sitting under one or more of the Commissions hereinafter mentioned. All or any of the said Commissions may be issued to any part of England, and at any time when her Majesty thinks proper.

[3] The said Commissions are :

(*a.*) A Commission of Oyer and Terminer, by which the Commissioners, or any two of them, of whom one of certain persons named must be one, are commanded to make diligent inquiry into all treasons, felonies, and misdemeanors whatever, committed within certain counties specified in the Commission, and to hear and determine the same according to law.

(*b.*) A Commission of Gaol Delivery, by which the Commissioners, or any two of them, of whom one of certain persons named must be one, are commanded to deliver a gaol or gaols specified in the said Commission.

(*c.*) A Commission of Assize and Nisi Prius, by which [4] the Commissioners are commanded to take all the assizes, juries,

---

[1] 36 & 37 Vict. c. 66, s. 31 (2).

[2] 1 Hist. Cr. Law, 85.

[3] The Commission of Oyer and Terminer applies only to cases where the indictment is found before the Commissioners. The Commission of Gaol Delivery enables them to try all persons in prison or on bail. The Commissions of Assize and Nisi Prius appear to apply only to nisi prius records. The Commission of the Peace seems to be superfluous, as it is to the same effect as the Commission of Oyer and Terminer, except that it is narrower. As to all these commissions see 1 Chitty Crim. Law, 141-151 ; and see the forms in 4 Chitty, 128-170. For the History of the Courts see 1 Hist. Cr. Law. ch. iv. pp. 75-144.

[4] Nothing is said as to a quorum. 4 Chitty, 137 ; but the writ of 'si non omnes,' mentioned in the last paragraph of Art. 24, meets this.

and certificates, before whatsoever justices arraigned,[1] since a time specified in the Commission, in certain counties specified in the Commission. [2] Such Commissioners have power to try all offences whatever which are sent down by the High Court to be tried before them as such Commissioners.

(*d.*) A Commission of the Peace, by which any two or more of the Commissioners are commanded amongst other things to inquire into, hear, and determine certain felonies and misdemeanors specified in the said Commission.

ARTICLE 24.

[3] OF THE PERSONS TO WHOM THE SAID COMMISSIONS ARE ISSUED. COMMISSIONS AND WRITS OF ASSOCIATION AND SI NON OMNES.

The said Commissions are issued upon fiats under her Majesty's sign-manual specifying the persons to whom they are to be issued on each circuit.

The Commission of Oyer and Terminer is issued to the Lord Chancellor, the Lord President of the Council, the Lord Privy Seal, and certain noblemen resident in the counties on the circuit, and in the case of each of the English circuits to two Judges, and in the case of each of the Welsh circuits to one Judge of the Supreme Court of Justice (liable to go circuit), and to all the Queen's Counsel and Serjeants-at-Law practising on the circuit, and to the Clerk of Assize, Clerk of Arraigns, Associate and Clerk of Indictments, who are collectively called the Associates.

The Commission directs that the matters mentioned in it shall be inquired into, heard, and determined by two at

---

[1] In the form given in 4 Chitty, 136, the Commission is to take all assizes since the reign of Queen Anne, the date of the form being 1802. I think it is now usual to date back to the end of the reign of George 3.

[2] This is the interpretation put by Hale (2 P. C. 40) on the statutes 27 Edw. 1, c. 3, and 14 Hen. 6, c. 1. As to the Commission of Nisi Prius, it is said in 1 Chitty Crim. Law, 146, to be annexed to the office of justices appointed under the Commission of Assize by 13 Edw. 1, c. 30. The old statutes have become very obscure, and the matter is only of antiquarian interest. See 1 Hist. Cr. Law.

[3] 4 Chitty Crim. Law, pp. 130a-139.

least of the persons named, of whom one of the Judges,
Queen's Counsel, and Serjeants aforesaid must be one
[¹ and one of the Associates another].

The Commissions of Assize and Gaol Delivery are addressed
to the same Judges, Queen's Counsel, and Serjeants, as the
Commissions of Oyer and Terminer, together with those whom
her Majesty has associated with them. The persons so
associated are the same as those named in the Commission of
Oyer and Terminer, and a Commission called a Commission of
Association is issued to the Associates commanding them to
associate themselves to the Commissioners of Gaol Delivery
and Assize, and a writ of association is directed to the
Commissioners of Gaol Delivery and Assize commanding
them to admit into their society the persons to whom the
said Commission of Association is issued.

A writ called a writ of *si non omnes* is also issued to the
Commissioners of ² Assize, and to the Associates, commanding
the said Commissioners and Associates, if they cannot all
conveniently be present at the execution of the Commission,
then that any two of them who shall happen to be present,
and of whom one of the Commissioners of Assize must be
one [and one of the Associates the other], shall execute the
Commission.

ARTICLE 25.

THE CENTRAL CRIMINAL COURT.

³ The Central Criminal Court is a Court of which the
following persons are the Judges; that is to say, the Lord
Mayor for the time being of the City of London, the Lord Chancellor or Lord Keeper of the Great Seal,⁴ all the Judges for the

---

¹ This is not stated in the Commission, but is a necessary consequence of the
merely complimentary nature of the appointment of the Chancellor, &c., and of
the practice of one commissioner sitting in each Court. There must be two to
make a quorum, and the circuit officers are the only persons left for the purpose.

² No mention of gaol delivery in Chitty.

³ 4 & 5 Will. 4, c. 36, s. 1; 1 Hist. Cr. Law, 118.

⁴ I suppose this is the effect of the Judicature Act of 1873. Till that Act was
passed the judges of the Court of Equity were not in the Commission of the
Central Criminal Court; the Judge of the Admiralty and the Dean of the Arches
were. Under 37 & 38 Vict. c. 85, s. 85, the judge appointed under the Public
Worship Regulation Act is *ex officio* Dean of the Arches.

time being of the High Court, the Judge of the Provincial Courts of Canterbury and York, the Aldermen of the City of London, the Recorder, the Common Serjeant, the Judges of the Sheriffs' Court of the City of London for the time being, and every person who has been Lord Chancellor, Lord Keeper, or a Judge of the High Courts, or of her Majesty's superior Courts at Westminster, together with such others as her Majesty from time to time appoints. [1] Her Majesty from time to time issues to the persons above mentioned a Commission of oyer and terminer, to inquire of, hear, and determine all treasons, murders, felonies, and misdemeanors committed within the district of the Central Criminal Court, and a Commission of gaol delivery, to deliver her Majesty's gaol of [2] Newgate of the prisoners therein.

ARTICLE 26.

THE COURT OF THE LORD HIGH ADMIRAL.

[3] The Court of the Lord High Admiral is a Court having jurisdiction over all offences to which the criminal law of England extends, committed on the high seas, or in ports, havens, creeks, and rivers below bridges where great ships go, either within the body of any English county or within the body of any foreign country or dominion of her Majesty.

The jurisdiction of the Admiral is exercised by the Courts hereinafter mentioned.

ARTICLE 27.

WHERE COURTS MAY SIT.

The House of Lords and the Court of the Lord High

---

[1] 4 & 5 Will. 4, c. 36, s. 2.

[2] In consequence of regulations made under the Prison Act, 1877, the gaol of Newgate is not now in use, but all enactments referring to the gaol of Newgate, save as may be prescribed, are construed to include and to have included the prison or prisons for the time being appointed by a rule of the Secretary of State made in pursuance of the Prison Act, 1877, as a prison or prisons to which prisoners who might otherwise be committed to Newgate may be committed, or in which prisoners triable at the Central Criminal Court are to be confined before or during trial or at either of such times. 44 & 45 Vict. c. 64, s. 2, subs. (2).

[3] For the History of the Admiral's Court and his Jurisdiction, see 2 Hist. Cr. Law, 16-26.

Steward may sit in England, and probably in any part of the United Kingdom.

The High Court (Queen's Bench Division) sits at Westminster Hall in the county of Middlesex, but may sit in any part of England or Wales.

The Courts of the Commissioners hereinbefore mentioned must sit for the purpose of executing their several commissions within each county for which it is to be executed, [1] provided that any commissioner before whom any court is holden by virtue of any of her Majesty's Commissions of assize, or nisi prius, oyer and terminer, or general gaol delivery, may hold such court for any county, and also for any county of a city, county of a town, borough, or other jurisdiction locally situate within or adjacent to such county, in any court-house or other building in or belonging to such county or county of a city or town indiscriminately, and may also adjourn any such court from or to any such building, provided that no such court may be held in any place more than three miles distant from the county or county corporate for which it is held.

[1] 2 & 3 Vict. c. 72 (condensed).

CHAPTER V.

OF JUSTICES OF THE PEACE—THEIR QUALIFICATION AND APPOINTMENT.

ARTICLE 28.

DUTIES OF A JUSTICE OF THE PEACE.

[1] THE duties of a Justice of the Peace are to keep the peace [2] within the district in which he is authorized to act, and to cause to be kept therein all ordinances and statutes for the good of the peace and for preservation of the same and for the quiet rule and government of the Queen's people, and to inquire into and hear and determine [3] such offences as fall within his jurisdiction as hereinafter mentioned, and to discharge all other duties imposed upon him by any statute.

ARTICLE 29.

APPOINTMENT AND REMOVAL OF JUSTICES OF THE PEACE.

All Justices of the Peace are appointed and may be dismissed by her Majesty.

All Justices of the Peace are appointed to act within certain districts hereinafter defined. If the district is a county or part of a county the justices appointed to act in it

---

[1] These words are taken from the form of the Commission given in 3 Burn. 111-112, and said to have been settled by the judges in 35 Eliz. (1593). For history of Justices of the Peace, see 1 Hist. Cr. Law, 111, 190.

[2] See Chapter VIII.

[3] The words of the Commission are "all felonies, poisonings, enchantments, sorceries, arts magic, trespasses, forestallings, regratings, ingrossings, and extortions whatsoever, and all and singular other crimes of which the justices of the peace may and ought lawfully to inquire." Then follow references to a great number of statutory powers of justices. Many of their duties have nothing to do with the criminal law; those which have are defined in various parts of this book.

C

are hereinafter called County Magistrates. If the district is a county corporate, city, or borough, the justices appointed to act in it are hereinafter called Borough Magistrates. Justices of the Peace appointed under the provisions of any statute and paid a salary for discharging their duties are hereinafter called Stipendiary Magistrates.

ARTICLE 30.

OF THE QUALIFICATION OF COUNTY MAGISTRATES.

No one is capable of being or acting as a County Magistrate unless he is qualified as follows :—

(*a.*) [1] By being a peer or lord of Parliament or the eldest son or heir-apparent of any peer or lord of Parliament, or of any person qualified to serve as a knight of the shire under 9 Anne, c. 5 ; or

(*b.*) [2] By having in possession for his own use or benefit an estate, either in law or in equity, for life or of inheritance, or an estate for a term of years determinable upon a life or lives, or which when originally created was for twenty-one years at least, in lands in England or Wales, of the clear yearly value of £100 over and above all incumbrances and charges, or the immediate reversion or remainder of or in lands leased for one, two, or three lives, or for a term of years determinable upon the death of one, two, or three lives, upon reserved rents, and which [lands] are of the yearly value of £300 ; or

---

[1] 5 Geo. 2, c. 18, s. 5. The statutes on this subject are complicated, and in the Revised Statutes they are made very obscure by the omission of the repealed parts of 5 Geo. 2, c. 18. They stand thus :—By 5 Geo. 2, c. 18, s. 1, a qualification of £100 a year in land was first required for magistrates. By s. 2 attorneys were disqualified, and a proviso was put into s. 5 exempting the eldest sons of peers, &c., from the statute. By 18 Geo. 2, c. 20, s. 1 of 5 Geo. 2, c. 18, was re-enacted, with the addition that a reversionary interest in £300 a year should be a qualification. By 34 & 35 Vict. c. 18 (Statute Law Revision Act of 1867), 5 Geo. 2, c. 18, s. 1, is repealed, and in the Revised Statutes the remains of the statute read as if it disqualified all persons not being the eldest sons of peers, &c. The qualification for a knight of the shire by 9 Anne, c. 5, was an estate in land of £600 a year.

[2] 18 Geo. 2, c. 20, s. 1.

(*c.*) [1] By having during the two years immediately preceding his appointment been the occupier of a dwelling-house assessed to the inhabited house duty at the value of not less than £100 within any county, riding, or division in England and Wales, and during that time having been rated to all rates and taxes in respect of the said premises.

[2] Every one who, not being so qualified, accepts or takes upon himself the office of a Justice of the Peace, or does any act as such, forfeits a sum of £100, half to the Queen and half to any informer who will sue therefor.

[3] This Article does not apply to any metropolitan magistrate as regards the counties mentioned in Article 32.

[4] Nor to the chief magistrate of the Metropolitan Police Court at Bow Street as regards the county of Berks.

[5] Nor to any County Court judge whose name is inserted by her Majesty in any commission of the peace for the county, riding, or division of a county for which he is appointed judge of the County Court.

[6] Nor to any person appointed to act as a Justice of the Peace in and for the Scilly Islands.

[7] Nor to the Harbour-master for the time being of the harbour of Holyhead in the event of its seeming meet to her Majesty to assign to him her Majesty's commission to act as a Justice of the Peace within the limits within which he is empowered to act in harbour matters.

---

[1] 38 & 39 Vict. c. 54, s. 1.

[2] 5 Geo. 2, c. 18, s. 3. The penalty does not in terms extend to disqualified persons acting as justices.

[3] 2 & 3 Vict. c. 71, s. 3.

[4] 11 & 12 Vict. c. 42, s. 31.

[5] 9 & 10 Vict. c. 95.

[6] 4 & 5 Will. 4, c. 43.

[7] 30 & 31 Vict. c. 124, s. 12. By 28 & 29 Vict. c. 124, s. 5, it is enacted that the superintendents of H.M. Dockyards shall be in all places justices of the peace in regard to all offences specified in that Act, and all matters relating to her Majesty's name, service, and the stores, provisions, and accounts thereof. The offences are the presentation of forged certificates (s. 6), and the personation of certain persons (s. 8). The Act says nothing about the qualification of the justices, which may be an accidental omission. If so, it is an unfortunate one, as it exposes every unqualified person who acts under the Act to the penalties stated in Article 30.

ARTICLE 31.

BOROUGH MAGISTRATES.

[1]The Mayor, and in boroughs, under 45 & 46 Vict. c. 50, where there is a recorder, the Recorder for the time being of every borough, is a Justice of the Peace in and for such borough, and the mayor continues to be such Justice of the Peace during the next succeeding year after he ceases to be mayor.

Every person elected to be mayor must declare, in the form specified in 45 & 46 Vict. c. 50, Schedule 8, form A, that he is seised or possessed of real or personal estate, or both, to the amount of £1000 over and above what will satisfy his just debts.

[2]Her Majesty may from time to time assign to any persons her commission to act as Justices of the Peace in and for each borough [3]having a separate commission of the peace, except the county of the City of London, provided that every person so assigned resides within the borough for which he is so assigned, or within seven miles of it or of some part of it, or occupies a house, warehouse, or other property in it during such time as he acts as a Justice of the Peace in and for such borough.

ARTICLE 32.

METROPOLITAN STIPENDIARY MAGISTRATES.

[4]Her Majesty has power to appoint any number of persons not exceeding twenty-seven to be magistrates of the Police Courts existing or to be established in the Metropolitan Police District.

Every such magistrate is by virtue of his appointment a Justice of the Peace for the counties of Middlesex, Surrey, Kent, Essex, and Hertfordshire, the city and liberty of Westminster and the liberty of the Tower of London.

---

[1] 45 & 46 Vict. c. 50, ss. 155, 163 ; 1 Hist. Cr. Law, 116.

[2] 45 & 46 Vict. c. 50, s. 157.

[3] 5 & 6 Will. 4, c. 76, Schedule A. This Act, the Municipal Corporations Act, 1835, is repealed by 45 & 46 Vict. c. 50, which applies (s. 6) to those places to which the repealed Act applied. The new Act comes into operation on January 1, 1883. 1 Hist. Cr. Law, 229–33.

[4] 2 & 3 Vict. c. 71, ss. 1, 3.

[1] The Chief Magistrate of the Metropolitan Police Court at Bow Street for the time being is also a Justice of the Peace for the county of Berks if his name is inserted in the Commission of the Peace for that county.

Every person so appointed must at the time of his appointment have practised as a barrister during at least seven years then last past, or as a barrister for four years then last past, having previously practised as a certificated special pleader for three years below the bar.

[2] Or must be a stipendiary magistrate acting for some city, town, liberty, borough, or place in England and Wales under Article 33.

ARTICLE 33.

OTHER STIPENDIARY MAGISTRATES.

[3] Her Majesty may appoint a person, being a barrister-at-law of seven years' standing, to be a police magistrate and a Justice of the Peace for any [4] borough, or a barrister of five years' standing to be such a magistrate for any [5] city or place with 25,000 inhabitants not included in any district for which a stipendiary magistrate is acting under any Act of Parliament, upon such by-laws and such provision as to his salary being made as are provided for by 45 & 46 Vict. c. 50, s. 161, and 26 & 27 Vict. c. 97, respectively.

ARTICLE 34.

PERSONS DISQUALIFIED FROM ACTING AS JUSTICES.

[6] No person is capable of becoming or being a Justice of

---

[1] 11 & 12 Vict. c. 42, s. 31.

[2] 21 & 22 Vict. c. 74, s. 13.

[3] 5 & 6 Will. 4, c. 76, s. 99 ; 26 & 27 Vict. c. 97.

[4] i.e., any place named in Schedule A or B of the Municipal Corporations Act, 5 & 6 Will. 4, c. 76, or under 45 & 46 Vict. c. 50.

[5] These words mean any city or place not a municipal corporation, wherein the Public Health Act, Local Government Act, or Local Improvement Act is in operation, and comprise the whole area to which such Acts extend. 26 & 27 Vict. c. 97, s. 2.

[6] 34 Vict. c. 18, s. 1. The exclusion was formerly larger ; see 6 & 7 Vict. c. 73, s. 33, and 5 Geo. 2, c. 18, s. 2. " County " means and includes a riding or division of a county having a separate commission of the peace. I have omitted some special disqualifications as to particular classes of cases, e.g., a mine-owner cannot sit in mining cases. 35 & 36 Vict. c. 76, s. 76.

the Peace for any county in England and Wales (not being a county of a city or county of a town) in which he practises and carries on the profession or business of a solicitor or proctor; and where any person practises and carries on such profession or business in any city or town being a county of itself, he is for the purpose of this Article deemed to carry on the same in the county within which such county or town or any part thereof is situate.

[1] No person exercising the office of Sheriff in any county may act as a Justice of the Peace in the county in which he is Sheriff and whilst he is Sheriff.

[2] If any person assigned by her Majesty's Commission to act as a Justice of the Peace is adjudged bankrupt, or makes any arrangement or composition with his creditors under the Bankruptcy Act, 1869, he becomes and remains incapable of acting as a Justice of the Peace until he has been newly assigned by her Majesty in that behalf.

ARTICLE 35.
MAGISTRATES IN THE CITY OF LONDON.

[3] The Lord Mayor of London, the Recorder of London, and all the Aldermen are Justices of the Peace for the City of London by virtue of charters granted to the City of London.

The Lord Mayor of London, the Recorder of London, and all the Aldermen who have passed the chair are Justices of the Peace for the borough of Southwark.

ARTICLE 36.
MAGISTRATES BY CHARTER.

[4] There are magistrates by charter in places which were municipal corporations before the Municipal Corporations Act of 1835 and are not within that Act.

[1] 1 Ma. st. 2, c. 8.
[2] 32 & 33 Vict. c. 62, s. 22. The disqualification of borough magistrates follows on their disqualification as mayors, aldermen, town-councillors, &c. See 32 & 33 Vict. c. 62, s. 21, applying to that Act 5 & 6 Will. 4, c. 76, ss. 52, 53.
[3] Municipal Corporation Commissioners' Report, pp. 77, 80. There is also a "Justice of the Bridge Yard," as to whom see p. 93.
[4] See 1. Hist. Crim. Law, 116-21.

CHAPTER VI.

OF COURTS OF QUARTER SESSION.

ARTICLE 37.

GENERAL QUARTER SESSIONS AND GENERAL SESSIONS.

[1] IT is the duty of the county magistrates named in any Commission of the Peace for any county, or part of a county, to hold Courts called the General Quarter Sessions of the Peace in the first week after the 11th day of October, the first week after the 28th day of December, the first week after the 31st day of March, and the first week after the 24th day of June.

[2] Provided that, in order to prevent the holding of the Spring Sessions from interfering with the holding of the Spring Assizes, the justices assembled in the Quarter Sessions next after the 28th December may (if there be occasion to do so) name two Justices of the Peace, and empower them, as soon as may be after the time for holding the Spring Assizes is appointed, to fix a day for holding the next General Quarter Sessions of the Peace not earlier than the 7th of March nor later than the 22nd of April.

Such Courts are hereinafter called County Quarter Sessions.

ARTICLE 38.

BOROUGH QUARTER SESSIONS.

[3] Her Majesty may grant a separate Court of Quarter

---

[1] 11 Geo. 4 & 1 Will. 4, c. 70, s. 35.

[2] 4 & 5 Will. 4, c. 47. When this Act was passed, the Spring Assizes were held in the spring. The present Spring Assizes are held much later than the old ones; but the old Spring Assizes correspond to the present Winter Assizes.

[3] 45 & 46 Vict. c. 50, ss. 162, 163, embodying 5 & 6 Will. 4, c. 76, s. 103, and 7 Will. 4 & 1 Vict. c. 78, ss. 49, 50 ; and see *Rutter* v. *Chapman*, 8 M. & W. 1, on the construction of the latter Act. For history of Court see 1 Hist. Cr. Law, 116.

Sessions to any of the boroughs named in Schedule A or B of the 5 & 6 Will. 4, c. 76, or to any borough incorporated under 7 Will. 4 & 1 Vict. c. 78, upon such provision being made for the payment of the salary of a Recorder as is in the said Acts mentioned. If such a grant is made, her Majesty may appoint a barrister of five years' standing to be Recorder of the borough, and to hold that office during good behaviour.

The Courts of Quarter Session held under and by virtue of any such grant are hereinafter called Borough Quarter Sessions.

ARTICLE 39.

THE JURISDICTION OF COURTS OF QUARTER SESSION IN CRIMINAL CASES.

The Courts of Quarter Session may try any person for any offence mentioned in the Commission of the Peace, or referred to by the general words contained in it [[1] but not, it is said, offences newly created by a statute, unless an authority be given to them by express words].

[2] They may not try treason, murder, any capital felony, any felony for which a person not previously convicted of felony is punishable by penal servitude for life, or

1. Misprision of treason.

2. Offences against the Queen's title, person, prerogative, or government, or against either House of Parliament.

3. Offences subject to the penalties of præmunire.

4. Blasphemy and offences against religion.

5. Administering or taking unlawful oaths.

6. Perjury and subornation of perjury.

7. Making or suborning any other person to make a false

---

[1] 2 Hawk. P. C. 47, quoting *R.* v. *James*, 2 Str. 1256; and see 1 Chitty, 139; 4 Steph. Com. 312. If this is the law, it seems to have fallen into disuse or neglect, for the Quarter Sessions in practice try all cases except those which they are forbidden to try either by 5 & 6 Vict. c. 38, s. 1, or by express words in the statute creating the offence. See the latter part of this Article. The Consolidation Acts of 1861 contain no express words authorizing the Quarter Sessions to try the large number of cases contained in them. The general words of the Commission are wide enough to cover anything.

[2] 5 & 6 Vict. c. 38, s. 1.

oath, affirmation, or declaration, punishable as perjury or as a misdemeanor.

8. Forgery.

9. Unlawfully and maliciously setting fire to crops of corn, grain, or pulse, or to any part of a wood, coppice, or plantation of trees, or to any heath, gorse, fern, or furze.

10. Bigamy and offences against the laws relating to marriage.

11. Abduction of women and girls.

12. Endeavouring to conceal the birth of a child.

13. [1] Any of the misdemeanors created by ss. 75–86, both inclusive, of 24 & 25 Vict. c. 96 (the Larceny Act).

14. Composing, printing, or publishing blasphemous, seditious, or defamatory libels.

15. [2] Bribery and undue influence.'

16. Unlawful combinations and conspiracies, except conspiracies or combinations to commit any offence which such justices or recorder respectively have or has jurisdiction to try when committed by one person.

17. Stealing or fraudulently taking or injuring or destroying records or documents belonging to any court of law or equity or relating to any proceeding therein.

18. Stealing or fraudulently destroying or concealing wills or testamentary papers, or any document or written instrument being or containing evidence of the title to any real estate or any interest in lands, tenements, and hereditaments.

19. [3] The offence of entering land, armed, by night, to the number of three or more, in pursuit of game.

20. [4] Personation, as defined by 37 & 38 Vict. c. 36, s. 3.

---

[1] 24 & 25 Vict. c. 96, s. 87. These are misappropriations by bankers, &c. See my Digest, ch. xli., Articles 343–350, both inclusive. In the 5 & 6 Vict. c. 37, No. 13 in the list consists of offences against the Bankruptcy law, but this was repealed by 31 & 32 Vict. c. 62, s. 20.

[2] 17 & 18 Vict. c. 102, s. 10; 5 & 6 Vict. c. 37, mentions bribery only.

[3] 9 Geo. 4, c. 69, s. 9; Digest, Article 77.

[4] 37 & 38 Vict. c. 36, s. 3; Digest, Article 367.

ARTICLE 40.

CONSTITUTION OF THE COUNTY COURTS OF QUARTER SESSION.

The magistrates in the Commission are the judges of the County Quarter Sessions.

[1] Provided that no metropolitan police magistrate is competent as such to act as one of the Justices of the Peace in Quarter Sessions assembled for any of the counties for which as such magistrate he is a justice; [2] nor is any magistrate of any borough within any county qualified as such to act as a Justice of the Peace for the county in Quarter Sessions assembled.

[3] The Court of Quarter Sessions continues during the continuance of the Commission of the Peace under which it sits. It may be adjourned to a different time and place from that at which it is required by law to assemble, provided that such time is not later than the next session required by law to be held; and it may adjourn the consideration of any particular matter to the next or any subsequent Court of Quarter Sessions unless it is required by statute to dispose of such matter at any particular sessions.

[4] Whenever any Court of County Quarter Sessions is assembled for the dispatch of business the justices there present may, if and when in their discretion they see fit so to do, appoint two or more justices, one of whom must be of the quorum, to form a second Court for the purpose of hearing and determining such business as may be referred to them.

---

[1] 2 & 3 Vict. c. 71, s. 14. In practice one of the magistrates is always chosen chairman. He sums up; but this is merely an arrangement for the dispatch of business. A paid assistant-judge and deputy assistant-judge are appointed for the Middlesex Sessions under 7 & 8 Vict. c. 71; 14 & 15 Vict. c. 55; 22 & 23 Vict. c. 4; 37 & 38 Vict. c. 7.

[2] 45 & 46 Vict. c. 50, s. 158.

[3] 2 Hawk. P. C. 64; Pritchard's Q. S. 28, 29.

[4] 21 & 22 Vict. c. 73, s. 9.

ARTICLE 41.

[1] The Recorder is the sole judge of a Borough Court of Quarter Sessions.

The Recorder of every borough must hold a Court of Quarter Sessions therein once in every quarter of a year, or oftener if and as he thinks fit or the Secretary of State directs.

[2] In case of sickness or unavoidable absence the Recorder of any borough may appoint by writing signed by him a barrister of five years' standing to act as Deputy Recorder at the Quarter Sessions then next ensuing or then being held, and not longer or otherwise. Such sessions are not illegal, nor are the acts of a Deputy-Recorder invalid by reason of the cause of the absence of the Recorder not being unavoidable.

[3] Whenever it appears to the Recorder [or other person presiding] at any Borough Quarter Sessions that the said Quarter Sessions are likely to last more than three days including the day of assembling, such Recorder or other person may in his discretion order a second court to be formed, and appoint by writing signed by him a barrister of not less than five years' standing, who is to be called the Assistant-Recorder, to preside and try such felonies and misdemeanors as shall be referred to him therein.

If at any time during the sitting of such second court the Recorder or other person is of opinion that it is no longer required, he may direct the Assistant-Recorder at a proper opportunity to adjourn it.

The power of appointing an Assistant-Recorder as aforesaid must not be exercised unless it has been before each

---

[1] 45 & 46 Vict. c. 50, s. 165. As to these Courts see 1 Hist. Cr. Law, 116–122.

[2] 45 & 46 Vict. c. 50, s. 166.

[3] 11 Will. 4 & 1 Vict. c. 19, and 45 & 46 Vict. c. 50, s. 168, as to boroughs within the Municipal Corporations Act 1882. These sections contain provisions as to subordinate officers, and as to the payment of the assistant-recorder, &c.

Quarter Session certified to him in writing by the mayor or two aldermen or the town clerk of the borough, that the council thereof have resolved that it will be expedient that the same be exercised ; nor unless the name of the barrister to be appointed has at some previous time been approved by the Secretary of State as that of a fit and proper person to be from time to time so appointed.

ARTICLE 42.

COURT TO BE OPENED AND ADJOURNED BY MAYOR IN RECORDER'S ABSENCE.

[1] In the absence of the Recorder and Deputy-Recorder, the mayor must, at the times for the holding of the Borough Courts of Quarter Session, open the Court, and adjourn the the holding thereof, and respite all recognizances conditioned for appearing thereat, until such day as he then and there, and so from time to time, causes to be proclaimed.

This power does not authorize the mayor to sit as a judge of the said Court for the trial of offenders, or to do any other act in the character of a judge of the Court.

[1] 45 & 46 Vict. c. 50, s. 167.

CHAPTER VII.

OF CORONERS.

ARTICLE 43.

DUTIES OF CORONERS.

A CORONER is an officer [1] whose duty it is to hold inquests upon the death of certain persons on the occasions and in the manner hereinafter mentioned, and also to hold inquests in cases of treasure trove.

ARTICLE 44.

DIFFERENT KINDS OF CORONERS.

[2] There are four kinds of Coroners—Official Coroners, Franchise Coroners, Coroners by election for counties, and Borough Coroners.

ARTICLE 45.

OFFICIAL CORONERS.

The Lord Chief Justice of England, and the Judges of the High Court of Justice are Official Coroners for the whole of England.

ARTICLE 46.

FRANCHISE CORONERS.

In many precincts particular persons are Coroners by franchise, or have the power of appointing Coroners for that precinct.

---

[1] See 1 Hist. Cr. Law, 216, 245. Coroners have other duties not connected with the administration of criminal justice.

[2] Jervis on Coroners, 2.

Illustrations.

The Mayor of London is by charter Coroner of London.
The Dean and Chapter of Westminster appoint a coroner for the city
and liberty of Westminster.

ARTICLE 47.

CORONERS BY ELECTION FOR COUNTIES.

There are in every county in England and Wales Coroners,
the number of whom is determined by custom, and who are
elected by the freeholders of the county.

ARTICLE 48.

INCREASE OF NUMBER OF CORONERS.

If the number of Coroners is insufficient for the transaction
of the business to be done, her Majesty may issue a writ *de
coronatore eligendo* requiring the freeholders of the county
to elect an additional Coroner or Coroners.

ARTICLE 49.

DIVISION OF COUNTIES INTO CORONERS' DISTRICTS.

[1] The Justices of the Peace for any county may, after
giving notice to all the Coroners in the county, and hearing
and conferring with them, petition her Majesty that the
county may be divided into two or more Coroners' districts,
or that any alteration may be made in any existing division
thereof.

[2] Her Majesty, with the advice of her Privy Council, may,
after taking into consideration any such petition, and any
petition by any Coroner of the county concerning such proposed division, order any such county to be divided into as
many districts as may seem expedient to her, and give them
names, and determine at what place in each district the Court
for the election of Coroner for such district shall be held.

[1] 7 & 8 Vict. c. 92, ss. 2 & 3 (compressed).
[2] Ibid. s. 4.

[1] Her Majesty may also make such an order if she issues a writ *de coronatore eligendo* without such a petition as aforesaid.

ARTICLE 50.

CORONERS ASSIGNED TO DISTRICTS.

[2] The Justices in Quarter Sessions must assign one of such districts to each of the persons holding the office of coroner.

ARTICLE 51.

ELECTION UPON A VACANCY.

[3] Upon the death, resignation or removal of any such person, and on all subsequent vacancies, a Coroner must be elected by the freeholders of the district. The Coroner must exercise the office of coroner within the district in and for which he is elected, and he must reside within such district, or in some place surrounded by it, or within two miles of its outer boundary. Every such person is a Coroner for the whole county to all intents and purposes. But he must not hold inquests out of his own district, except in case of the illness, incapacity, or unavoidable absence of the Coroner of any other district, or during the vacancy in his office, on which occasions he may hold inquests in such district, but if he does so he must in his inquisition certify the cause of his holding such inquest.

ARTICLE 52.

ELECTIONS, HOW HELD.

[4] The elections of Coroners are held at special County Courts convened by the Sheriff within not less than seven, nor more than fourteen, days from the receipt of the writ *de coronatore eligendo*. A poll, if demanded, may be held for two days, and for eight hours, terminating not later than 4 p.m. on each day.

[1] This seems to be the effect of words in s. 4.
[2] 7 & 8 Vict. c. 92, s. 5.
[3] Ibid.
[4] Sections 9–16.

ARTICLE 53.

DEPUTY-CORONER.

[1] Every Coroner of any county, city, riding, liberty, or division must by writing under his hand and seal nominate and appoint from time to time a fit and proper person—such appointment being subject to the approval of the Lord Chancellor—to act for him as his deputy in the holding of inquests.

A duplicate of the appointment must be forthwith transmitted to the clerk of the peace for the district in which the Coroner resides.

No deputy may act for any such Coroner except during the illness of such Coroner, or during his absence for any lawful or reasonable cause.

Any such appointment may at any time be revoked by the Coroner by whom it was made.

ARTICLE 54.

CORONER NOT TO ACT AS SOLICITOR IN CASES WHERE INQUEST HELD BEFORE HIM.

[2] In cases in which any person is charged by any coroner's inquisition with the commission of any crime, and is subsequently put upon his trial either on such inquisition or in pursuance of any bill of indictment found by the same, the Coroner before whom the inquisition was found shall be wholly incompetent to act as solicitor in prosecution or defence of such person for such crime either by himself or by his partner, directly or indirectly; and in all cases in which it appears to the judge before whom such person is tried, that any coroner has so acted, the judge must impose upon the coroner a fine not exceeding £50.

[1] 6 & 7 Vict. c. 83, s. 1.
[2] 7 & 8 Vict. c. 92, s. 18.

ARTICLE 55.

SALARIES OF COUNTY CORONERS.

[1] Every County Coroner is paid by a salary quarterly out of the county rate, the amount of which salary was originally fixed at not less than the average amount of fees, mileage, and allowances received by the Coroner or his predecessors for five years next before 31st of December, 1859; and such salary has since been subject to revision at the end of every five years.

ARTICLE 56.

REMOVAL OF COUNTY CORONERS.

[2] The Lord Chancellor may, if he thinks fit, remove for inability or misbehaviour in his office any County Coroner.

Any freeholders, justices, or other persons interested in any county may present a petition to the Lord Chancellor praying for the removal of any Coroner upon any ground showing that he is unable or unfit to discharge the duties of his office, and upon the hearing of such petition the Lord Chancellor may issue to the Sheriff of the county a writ for removing such Coroner (*de coronatore amovendo*), and a writ for choosing a new Coroner (*de coronatore eligendo*).

ARTICLE 57.

REMOVAL OF CORONERS ON CONVICTION.

[3] If any Coroner who is not appointed by virtue of an annual election or nomination, or whose office of Coroner is not annexed to any other office, is lawfully convicted of extortion or wilful neglect of his duty or misdemeanor in his office, the Court before whom he is so convicted may adjudge that he shall be removed from his office; and thereupon, if such Coroner was elected by the freeholders of any county, a

---

[1] 23 & 24 Vict. c. 116, s. 4.
[2] Ibid. s. 6.
[3] 25 Geo. 2, c. 29. s. 6.

D

writ must issue for the removing him from his office and electing another Coroner in his stead in such manner as writs for the removal or discharge of coroners and for electing coroners in their stead were in any cases directed by law before the passing of 25 Geo. 2, c. 29; and if the Coroner so convicted was appointed by the lord or lords of any liberty or franchise, or in any other manner than by the election of the freeholders of any county, the lord or lords of such liberty or franchise, or the person or persons entitled to the nomination or appointment of any such Coroner must, upon notice of such judgment of removal, nominate and appoint another person to be Coroner in his stead.

ARTICLE 58.

APPOINTMENT OF BOROUGH CORONERS.

[1] The council of a borough having a separate Court of Quarter Sessions must, within ten days next after receipt of the grant thereof by the council, appoint a fit person, not an alderman or councillor of the borough, to be Coroner of the borough. Thereafter no person other than the Coroner so appointed may take in the borough any inquisition belonging to the office of Coroner. Such Coroner holds office during good behaviour. A vacancy in the office must be filled up within ten days after it occurs. [2] On or before the 1st of February in every year such Coroner must send to the Secretary of State a return in writing, in such form as the Secretary of State directs, of the particulars of each case in which such Coroner or his deputy was called upon to hold an inquest during the year ending on the then last 31st of December.

ARTICLE 59.

BOROUGH CORONER'S DEPUTY.

[3] In case of illness or unavoidable absence, the Borough Coroner must appoint by writing signed by him a fit person,

---

[1] 45 & 46 Vict. c. 50, s. 171.
[2] Ibid. s. 173.
[3] Ibid. s. 172.

being a barrister or a solicitor of the High Court of Justice, and not an alderman or councillor of the borough, to act for him as Deputy-Coroner during his illness or un-avoidable absence, but no longer or otherwise. The mayor or two justices for the borough must, on each occasion, certify in writing signed by him or them, the necessity for the appointment of a Deputy-Coroner. This certificate must state the cause of absence of the Coroner, and must be openly read to every inquest jury summoned by the Deputy-Coroner.

ARTICLE 60.

COUNTY CORONERS ACT IN BOROUGHS WHICH HAVE NO CORONER.

[1] Where a borough has not a separate Court of Quarter Sessions no person other than the Coroner for the county or district in which the borough is situate, shall take in the borough any inquisition belonging to the office of Coroner. That Coroner is, for every inquisition duly taken by him within the borough, entitled to such rateable fees and salary as would be allowed and due to him, and to be allowed and paid in like manner, as for any other inquisition taken by him within the county or district.

---

[1] 45 & 46 Vict. c. 50, s. 174.

CHAPTER VIII.

TERRITORIAL DIVISION OF ENGLAND FOR ADMINISTRATION OF CRIMINAL JUSTICE.

ARTICLE 61.

COUNTIES AND CIRCUITS.

[1] THE English and Welsh counties are divided into eight circuits as set out in the note hereto.

[1] SOUTH-EASTERN CIRCUIT.

Hertfordshire.	Huntingdon.
Essex.	Cambridge.
Sussex.	Suffolk.
Kent.	Norfolk.

MIDLAND CIRCUIT.

Bedfordshire.	Northamptonshire.
Buckinghamshire.	Nottinghamshire.
Derbyshire.	Rutlandshire.
Leicestershire.	Warwickshire.
Lincolnshire.	

NORTHERN CIRCUIT.

Cumberland.	Lancashire.
Westmoreland.	

NORTH-EASTERN CIRCUIT.

Durham.	Yorkshire.
Northumberland.	

OXFORD CIRCUIT.

Berkshire.	Shropshire.
Oxfordshire.	Herefordshire.
Worcestershire.	Monmouthshire.
Staffordshire.	Gloucestershire.

WESTERN CIRCUIT.

Hampshire.	Cornwall.
Wiltshire.	Somerset.
Dorsetshire.	County of City of Bristol.
Devonshire.	

[1] Every part of a county which is detached from the main body of such county is considered for all purposes connected with the administration of criminal justice as forming part of that county by which it is surrounded.

[2] Every county of a city or town corporate (except London and Bristol) which is not itself the assize town for the county in which it is included, or to which it is adjacent, is for purposes of commitment and trial taken to be a part of the county in which it is included or to which it is adjacent.

[3] The towns of Berwick-on-Tweed and Newcastle-on-Tyne are adjacent for this purpose to the county of Northumberland, and the town of Hull to the county of York.

Separate commissions are issued for those counties of cities

NORTH WALES CIRCUIT.

Montgomeryshire.	Denbighshire.
Merionethshire.	Flintshire.
Carnarvonshire.	Cheshire.
Anglesey.	

SOUTH WALES CIRCUIT.

Pembrokeshire.	Glamorganshire.
Cardiganshire.	Brecon.
Caermarthenshire.	Radnorshire.

Middlesex (not included in any circuit).

Surrey, separate commission for.

Counties corporate, enumerated in 5 & 6 Will. 4, c. 76, s. 61. As to Berwick see s. 109.

Bristol.	Norwich.
Berwick-on-Tweed.	Worcester.
Canterbury.	York.
Chester.	Caermarthen.
Coventry.	Haverfordwest.
Exeter.	Hull.
Gloucester.	Newcastle-on-Tyne.
Lichfield.	Nottingham.
Lincoln.	Poole.
London.	Southampton.

[1] Effect of 2 & 3 Will. 4, c. 64, s. 26, and 7 & 8 Vict. c. 61, s. 1.

[2] Effect of 14 & 15 Vict. c. 55, s. 19.

[3] 14 & 15 Vict. c. 55, s. 24; 5 & 6 Will. 4, c. 76, s. 109 and Sched. C. And see Sched. D. to 45 & 46 Vict. c. 50. This schedule also provides that Bristol, Chester, and Exeter shall be deemed to be adjacent to Gloucestershire, Cheshire, and Devonshire respectively; but all these are assize towns.

or towns corporate which are assize towns for the counties in which they are included or to which they are adjacent, and a separate commission is issued for the county of the city of Bristol.

[1] Her Majesty may by order in Council provide in such manner, and subject to such regulations as to her Majesty may seem meet, for the discontinuance, either temporarily or permanently, wholly or partially, of any existing circuit, and the formation of any new circuit by the union of any counties or parts of counties, or partly in the one way and partly in the other, or by the constitution of any county or part of a county to be a circuit by itself.

ARTICLE 62.

ASSIZE COUNTIES.

Her Majesty may by order in Council from time to time unite any neighbouring counties together into one assize county for the purpose of any Court of Assize or Sessions of Oyer and Terminer or Gaol Delivery held in the months of [2] September, October,[3] November, December, January,[4] March, April, or May, and may appoint the places at which assizes are to be held for such counties.

[5] Her Majesty may by order in Council provide in such manner as may seem meet for the jurisdiction of the Court, and the attendance, jurisdiction, authority, and duty of sheriffs, gaolers, officers, jurors and other persons, the use of any prison, the removal of prisoners, the alteration of any commissions, writs, precepts, indictments, recognizances, proceedings and documents, the transmission of recognizances, inquisitions and documents, and the expenses of prosecutors and witnesses, and of maintaining and removing prisoners so far as may seem to her Majesty necessary for carrying into effect an order in Council under the Winter Assizes Act, 1876; and for any

---

[1] 37 & 38 Vict. c. 83, s. 23 (part). This power practically supersedes a more limited power of the same sort given by 26 & 27 Vict. c. 127.

[2] 40 & 41 Vict. c. 46.

[3] 39 & 40 Vict. c. 57, s. 2.

[4] 42 Vict. c. 1, s. 1.

[5] 39 & 40 Vict. c. 57, s. 2, sub-ss. (3) & (4).

matters which appear to her Majesty to be necessary or proper for carrying into effect an order in Council under the said Act.

[1] Her Majesty may by order in Council direct that the jurisdiction of the Central Criminal Court, at any session held for the Central Criminal Court district in the months of November, December, or January, shall extend to any neighbouring county or part of a county mentioned in the order as if it were included within the limits of the Central Criminal Court district, and may apply the Central Criminal Court Act to the said county or part of a county, and offences committed therein, as if the same were a county or part of a county mentioned in that Act.

ARTICLE 63.

DISTRICT OF THE CENTRAL CRIMINAL COURT.

The City of London, the county of Middlesex, and those parts of the counties of Essex, Kent, and Surrey which are within the [2] parishes and other places mentioned in the footnote hereto, are the district of the Central Criminal Court.

[1] 39 & 40 Vict. c. 57, s. 5.
[2] 4 & 5 Will. 4, c. 36, s. 2.

Essex.

Barking.	Walthamstow.
East Ham.	Wanstead, St. Mary.
West Ham.	Woodford.
Little Ilford.	Chingford.
Low Layton.	

Kent.

Charlton.	Plumstead.
Lee.	St. Nicholas, Deptford.
Lewisham.	Part of St. Paul's, Deptford, which
Greenwich.	is in Kent.
Woolwich.	Kidbrook (liberty).
Eltham.	Mottingham.

Surrey.

The borough of Southwark.	St. Mary, Newington.
Battersea.	Rotherhithe.
Bermondsey.	Streatham.
Camberwell.	Barnes.
Christchurch.	Putney.
Clapham.	Surrey part of St. Paul's, Dept-
Lambeth.	ford.

ARTICLE 64.

COMMISSIONS OF THE PEACE.

There are in England sixty-five Commissions of the Peace for counties, parts of counties, and liberties, namely:

One for each county in England, other than York and Lincoln	50
One for each riding of Yorkshire	3
One for each part of Lincolnshire	3
One for each of the following liberties :—Cawood, Cinque Ports, Ely, Haverfordwest, Peterborough, Ripon, St. Albans, Tower of London, Westminster . . .	9
	65

There are also Commissions of the Peace for each of the boroughs named in Schedules A and B of the Municipal Corporations Act, 1835, and for each of the boroughs incorporated subsequently under 7 Will. 4 & 1 Vict. c. 78.

ARTICLE 65.

LOCAL AUTHORITY OF MAGISTRATES DEPENDS ON THEIR COMMISSIONS.

Magistrates can act only within the limits assigned to them by the Commissions of the Peace in which they are named, or, in the case of Magistrates by Charter, within the limits of their charter, or, in the case of the City of London, within the City of London and the borough of Southwark, except in the cases hereinafter expressly excepted.

Tooting.	Kew.
Graveney.	Richmond.
Wandsworth.	Wimbledon.
Merton.	Clink (liberty).
Mortlake.	Lambeth Palace.

ARTICLE 66.

WHEN COUNTY MAGISTRATES EXCLUDED BY BOROUGH COMMISSION AND WHEN NOT.

[1] The County Magistrates of a county in which is situated a borough having a separate Commission of the Peace have in and for such borough concurrent jurisdiction with the Borough Magistrates. But if there is within any such borough a separate Court of Quarter Sessions, the jurisdiction of the Borough Magistrates within such borough is exclusive.

[1] 45 & 46 Vict. c. 50, s. 154, and see 5 & 6 Will. 4, c. 76, s. 111. (I think this is the meaning, or at least the effect, of the section.)

CHAPTER IX.

ARTICLE 67.

THE HOUSE OF LORDS AND THE COURT OF THE LORD HIGH STEWARD.

THE House of Lords and the Court of the Lord High Steward have jurisdiction over offences as to which their jurisdiction is exclusive in whatever part of the United Kingdom they are committed, or if they are committed out of the United Kingdom if the criminal law of England extends to them.

ARTICLE 68.

THE HOUSE OF LORDS ON AN IMPEACHMENT.

The House of Lords has jurisdiction over offences in respect of which the offender is impeached by the House of Commons wherever they may have been committed.

ARTICLE 69.

HIGH COURT OF JUSTICE.

The High Court of Justice (Queen's Bench Division) has jurisdiction over offences committed in any part of England. If such offence is committed in [2] Middlesex or in any other county in which the High Court is sitting, its jurisdiction over such an offence is immediate, and a bill may be found before it in the grand jury of the county.

If any offence is committed in any other county the High

---

[1] 1 Hist. Cr. Law, 276, and 2 Hist. Cr. Law, 9.
[2] Practically the Court of King's Bench has always sat in Middlesex, with an exception during the civil wars, and on one occasion during the plague.

Court of Justice may assume jurisdiction over it by the writ of *certiorari*, as hereinafter mentioned.

ARTICLE 70.

COLONIAL AND INDIAN CASES.

The Queen's Bench Division of the High Court of Justice has jurisdiction over all offences committed in India or the colonies which render the offender liable to be tried in England under 11 Will. 3, c. 12, or 13 Geo. 3, c. 63, s. 39, or 42 Geo. 3, c. 85.

ARTICLE 71.

LOCAL JURISDICTION OF COURTS OF OYER AND TERMINER AND GAOL DELIVERY.

Courts of Oyer and Terminer and Gaol Delivery have jurisdiction over all offences which they are otherwise competent to try, and which are committed within the limits of any county to which the Commission of Oyer and Terminer extends, and within which it is being executed. The Central Criminal Court has jurisdiction over all offences which it is otherwise competent to try, committed within its district.

ARTICLE 72.

JURISDICTION OF COUNTY COURT OF ASSIZE IN COUNTIES OF CITIES.

[1] Any prosecutor may prefer a bill of indictment for any offence committed or charged to be committed within the county of any city or town corporate to the jury of the county next adjoining to the county of such city or town corporate sworn and charged to inquire for the Queen for the body of such adjoining county at any Sessions of Oyer and Terminer or General Gaol Delivery, [[2] and every such indictment if found to be a true bill may be heard or determined before the justices

---

[1] 38 Geo. 3, c. 52, s. 2.
[2] This is not said in words, but is necessarily implied by other parts of the Act. See, e.g., s. 8.

of oyer and terminer or general gaol delivery for such county].

ARTICLE 73.

LOCAL JURISDICTION OF COURTS OF QUARTER SESSION.

Courts of Quarter Session have jurisdiction over all offences which they are otherwise competent to try, committed within the limits of the Commission of the Peace or charter under which the Justices or Recorder act.

ARTICLE 74.

LOCAL JURISDICTION OF THE ADMIRAL.

[1] The Admiral has jurisdiction over all offences to which the criminal law of England extends, committed

(*a.*) On the high sea, or

(*b.*) On any landlocked water within the body of any English county, or on any port, creek, haven, or navigable river below bridges where great ships go, or

(*c.*) On any landlocked water within the body of any foreign country, or on any port, creek, haven, or navigable river below bridges where great ships go in any such country.

In case (*a*) the jurisdiction of the Admiral is exclusive except in regard of the part of the land over which the tide flows and reflows, as to which the Admiral has jurisdiction when the tide is in, and the Courts of Common Law when it is out.

In case (*b*) the jurisdiction of the Admiral is concurrent with that of the Courts of Common Law.

In case (*c*) the jurisdiction of the Admiral is concurrent with the jurisdiction of the foreign Courts having jurisdiction in such places.

ARTICLE 75.

ADMIRALTY JURISDICTION OF CENTRAL CRIMINAL COURT.

[2] The Central Criminal Court may inquire of, hear, and determine any offence alleged to have been committed within

---

[1] Authorities and history in 2 Hist. Cr. Law, 16.

[2] 4 & 5 Will. 4, c. 36, s. 22.

the jurisdiction of the Admiralty of England, and deliver the gaol of Newgate of any person committed to or detained therein for any offence alleged to have been committed within that jurisdiction. ·

ARTICLE 76.

ADMIRALTY JURISDICTION OF COURTS OF OYER AND TERMINER AND GAOL DELIVERY.

[1] Her Majesty's Justices of Assize and others her Majesty's Commissioners by whom is holden any Court of oyer and terminer or general gaol delivery, may inquire into, hear, and determine all offences committed within the local jurisdiction of the Admiral, and deliver the gaols within the limits of their jurisdiction of persons committed to or imprisoned therein for any offence alleged to have been committed within such limits.

ARTICLE 77.

ADMIRALTY JURISDICTION UNDER CONSOLIDATION ACT, 1861.

All indictable offences mentioned in any of the following Acts, that is to say, the Larceny Act, 1861 (24 & 25 Vict. c. 96), the Malicious Mischief Act, 1861 (24 & 25 Vict. c. 97), the Forgery Act, 1861 (24 & 25 Vict. c. 98), the Coinage Offences Act, 1861 (24 & 25 Vict. c. 99), the Offences against the Person Act, 1861 (24 & 25 Vict. c. 98, s. 100), committed within the jurisdiction of the Admiralty of England or Ireland are deemed to be offences of the same nature and liable to the same punishments as if they had been committed upon the land in England or Ireland, and may be dealt with, inquired of, heard, and determined in any county or place in England or Ireland in which the offender is apprehended or is in custody, in the same manner in all respects as if they had been actually committed in that country or place.

---

[1] 7 & 8 Vict. c. 2, s. 1. As this statute, and the others hereinafter mentioned, supersede the earlier statutes of 28 Hen. 8, c. 15, and 39 Geo. 3, c. 37, I have not abstracted these Acts, though they are still in force. The whole history of the matter is given in 2 Hist. Cr. Law, chapter xvi. p. 16.

Article 78.

Admiralty Jurisdiction under Merchant Shipping Acts of 1854 and 1855.

[1] All offences against property or person committed in or at any place, either ashore or afloat, out of her Majesty's dominions by any master, seaman, or apprentice who at the time when the offence is committed is or within three months previously has been employed in any British ship are deemed to be offences of the same nature respectively, and are liable to the same punishments respectively, and may be inquired of, heard, tried, and determined and adjudged in the same manner, and by the same Courts and in the same places, as if such offences had been committed within the jurisdiction of the Admiralty of England.

[2] If any person, being a British subject, charged with having committed any crime or offence on board any British ship on the high seas, or in any foreign port or harbour, or if any person, being a British subject, charged with having committed any crime or offence on board any British ship on the high seas, is found within the jurisdiction of any court of justice in her Majesty's dominions which would have had cognizance of such crime or offence if committed within the limits of its ordinary jurisdiction, such Court has jurisdiction to hear and try the case as if such crime or offence had been committed within such limits.

[1] 17 & 18 Vict. c. 104, s. 267.
[2] 18 & 19 Vict. c. 91, s. 21.

CHAPTER X.

[1] *LOCAL JURISDICTION IN RESPECT OF CERTAIN SPECIAL OFFENCES, AND OFFENCES COMMITTED UNDER SPECIAL CIRCUMSTANCES.*

ARTICLE 79.

OFFENCES COMMITTED WITHIN 500 YARDS OF BOUNDARY OR PARTLY IN DIFFERENT COUNTIES.

[2] WHERE any felony or misdemeanor is committed on the boundary or boundaries of two or more counties or within the distance of 500 yards of any such boundary or boundaries, or is [3] begun in one county and completed in another, the offender may be tried in any of the said counties.

ARTICLE 80.

DEATH IN ENGLAND CAUSED BY INJURIES INFLICTED AT SEA AND VICE VERSÂ.

[4] Where any person being feloniously stricken, poisoned, or otherwise hurt upon the sea, or at any place out of England or Ireland, dies of such stroke, poisoning, or hurt in England or Ireland, or being feloniously stricken, poisoned, or hurt at any place in England or Ireland, dies of such stroke, poisoning, or hurt upon the sea, or at any place out of England or Ireland, every offence committed in respect of any such case may be dealt with, inquired of, tried,

[1] 1 Hist. Cr. Law, 276, and 2 Hist. Cr. Law, 16.

[2] 7 Geo. 4, c. 64, s. 12.

[3] This applies *inter alia* to a wound in one county and death in another, and generalizes and supersedes 2 & 3 Edw. 6, c. 24, which was repealed by 7 Geo. 4, c. 64. See *R.* v. *Jones,* 1 Russ. Cr. p. 8.

[4] 24 & 25 Vict. c. 100, s. 10. This section was required, notwithstanding 7 Geo. 4, c. 64, s. 12, because that section applies only to crimes committed partly in each of two or more counties; and the high sea is in no county.

determined, and punished in the county or place in England or Ireland in which such death, stroke, poisoning, or hurt happens.

ARTICLE 81.

TREASON AND CONSPIRACY.

[1] Persons charged with high treason or conspiracy may be prosecuted in any county in which any overt act charged in the indictment and done by any one of the traitors or conspirators can be proved to have been done.

ARTICLE 82.

LARCENY.

[2] If a person commits larceny in one county, and carries the goods with him through or into another, [3] with the continued intention of stealing, he may be tried either in the county in which he took the goods or in any county through or into which he so took them.

[4] If he commits compound larceny in one county, and carries the goods with him into any other with the continued intention of stealing them, he may be tried for the simple or compound larceny in the county where he took the goods, or for the simple larceny in any county into which he carried them, and he may be tried for the compound larceny in any of the counties into which he carried the goods if the circumstances constituting the aggravation continued during the carrying into such county, but not otherwise.

[5] If the nature of the goods is changed, he cannot in any case be tried for the larceny in any county into which he carried them after such change took place.

[6] This article does not apply to any larceny which would

[1] Archb. 38.

[2] Archb. 36; *R.* v. *Parkins*, 1 Moo. C. C. 45. All the rules stated in this article are rules at common law, and have been practically superseded by 24 & 25 Vict. c. 96, s. 114. See Art. 84.

[3] *R.* v. *Simmonds*, 1 Moo. C. C. 408.

[4] 1 Hale, 507; 2 Hale, 163; *R.* v. *Thompson*, 2 Russ. 174.

[5] *R.* v. *Edwards*, R. & R. 497; *R.* v. *Halloway*, 1 C. & P. 127.

[6] See cases collected in Archbold, H. 37 (ed. 1878).

not have been larceny at common law, or which is committed under such circumstances that the common law would not have punished it.

Illustrations.

1. A steals a watch in Middlesex and carries it into Surrey. A may be tried either in Middlesex or in Surrey.

2. A steals a watch from the person of B in Middlesex, and carries it into Surrey. A may be tried for stealing from the person in Middlesex, or for simple larceny in Surrey.

3. A steals a horse in Middlesex and rides it into Surrey. A may be tried for stealing a horse either in Middlesex or in Surrey.

4. A steals a watch in Middlesex, and being arrested there asks the policeman to accompany him into Surrey for some innocent purpose, and carries the watch into Surrey for that purpose. A may be tried in Middlesex, but not in Surrey.

5. A steals a watch in Middlesex and carries it into Surrey, where he breaks up the watch, and melts the gold into an ingot. He carries the gold into Kent. He may be tried either in Middlesex or Surrey, but not in Kent.

6. A rips lead from a roof in Middlesex and carries it into Surrey. A cannot be tried for larceny in Surrey under this Article (but see Art. 84).

7. A steals money in Edinburgh and carries it to Newcastle-on-Tyne. A cannot be tried at Newcastle-on-Tyne for larceny under this Article (but see Art. 84).

8. A steals money at sea and brings it to Middlesex. A cannot be tried in Middlesex either under this Article or under Art. 84, (but he might be tried in Middlesex under Art. 77).

ARTICLE 83.

RECEIVING STOLEN GOODS.

[1] When any one receives any chattel, money, valuable security, or other property whatsoever, knowing the same to have been feloniously or unlawfully stolen, taken, obtained, converted, or disposed of, the offender may be tried in any county or place in which he has or has had any such property in his possession, or in any county or place in which the party guilty of the principal felony or misdemeanor may by law be tried, whether such person receiving the goods is charged as an accessory after the fact

---

[1] 24 & 25 Vict. c. 96, s. 96.

E

to the felony, or with a substantive felony, or with a misdemeanor only.

ARTICLE 84.

HAVING OR RECEIVING IN ANY PART OF THE UNITED KINGDOM GOODS STOLEN IN ANOTHER PART.

[1] If any person has in his possession in any one part of the United Kingdom any chattel, money, valuable security, or any other property whatsoever which he has stolen or otherwise feloniously taken, or has or receives in any one part of the United Kingdom any chattel, money, valuable security, or other property whatsoever, knowing such property to have been stolen or otherwise feloniously taken, he may be tried in that part of the United Kingdom where he so has or receives such property.

ARTICLE 85.

ACCESSORIES TO FELONY.

[2] Any person charged with being accessory before or after the fact to any felony wholly committed within England or Ireland may be tried by any Court which has jurisdiction to try

the principal felony, or

any felonies committed in any county or place in which the act by reason whereof such person became such accessory was committed.

Any accessory before or after the fact to any other felony may be tried by any Court which has jurisdiction to try

the principal felony, or

any felonies committed in any county or place in which such person is apprehended, or is in custody.

---

[1] 24 & 25 Vict. c. 96, s. 114. To a great extent this is identical with Article 82, but it covers cases which were not larceny at common law, as well as stealing in Scotland or Ireland and carrying into England. It does not apply to thefts at sea, because they are already provided for. Thefts in the Channel Islands, or committed abroad, cannot be dealt with in England, even if the property is brought here.

[2] 24 & 25 Vict. c. 94, s. 7.

Illustrations.

A in Middlesex instigates B to commit murder in Surrey. A may be tried either in Middlesex or in Surrey.

A in Middlesex instigates B to commit murder on the high sea. A may be tried either by any Court having jurisdiction to try murders committed at sea, or by any Court having jurisdiction over murder at the place where A happens to be apprehended or to be in custody (i.e. every Court competent to try murder has by two different titles jurisdiction to try A).

ARTICLE 86.

OFFENCES COMMITTED UPON A JOURNEY.

[1] Where any felony or misdemeanor is committed on any person, or on or in respect of any property, in or upon any coach, waggon, cart, or other carriage whatever employed in any journey,

or is committed on any person, or on or in respect of any property, on board any vessel whatever employed on any voyage or journey upon any navigable river, canal, or inland navigation,

the offender may be tried in any county through any part whereof such coach, waggon, cart, carriage, or vessel passed in the course of the journey or voyage during which such offence was committed.

If the side, centre, or other part of any highway, or the side, bank, centre, or other part of any such river, canal, or navigation constitutes the boundary of any two counties, the offender may be tried in either of the said counties through or adjoining to or by the boundary of any part whereof such coach, waggon, cart, carriage, or vessel passed in the course of the journey or voyage during which such offence was committed.

ARTICLE 87.

CERTAIN OTHER OFFENCES.

Persons indicted for the offences mentioned in the first column of the Schedule hereto may, by virtue of the

---

[1] 7 Geo. 4, c. 64, s. 13.

E 2

statutory enactment referred to in the third column, be tried in the district specified in the second column.

SCHEDULE.

Bigamy . . .	Any county or place where the offender is apprehended or is in custody.	24 & 25 Vict. c. 100, s. 57.
Coinage. Tendering, uttering, or putting off any false or counterfeit coin committed in different districts within ten days of each other by the same person ; or any offence against Coinage Act by any persons acting in concert with each other.	Any district in which any such offence was committed.	24 & 25 Vict. c. 99, s. 28.
Convict being unlawfully at large after a sentence of transportation or penal servitude.	The county in which he is apprehended, or that from whence he was ordered to be transported or sent to penal servitude.	5 Geo. 4, c. 84, s. 22 ; and 20 & 21 Vict. c. 3, s. 3.
Foreign Enlistment Act offences.	The place in which the offence was wholly or partly committed, or any place in her Majesty's dominions in which the person who committed such offence may be. The venue in the margin to be that of the place of trial, and local description, if required, to be "In her Majesty's dominions."	34 & 35 Vict. c. 90, ss. 16, 17.
Forgery (any offence under any statute, or at common law).	Any county or place in which the offender is apprehended or is in custody.	24 & 25 Vict. c. 98, s. 41.
Inciting soldiers to mutiny.	Any county.	37 Geo. 3, c. 70, s. 2.
Larceny by person in the public service.	Any county in which he is apprehended or in custody, or in which the offence was committed.	24 & 25 Vict. c. 96, s. 70.
Merchant Shipping Act offences.	Any place where the offender may be.	17 & 18 Vict. c. 104, s. 520.

Post Office offences.	Any county or place where the offence was committed, or where the offender is apprehended or is in custody, or through or adjoining to which any person or any mail, letter, parcel, or post-bag, &c., in respect of which the offence was committed, passed in due course of conveyance or delivery by post.	7 Wm. 4 & 1 Vict. c. 36, s. 37.
Revenue offences and assaulting excise officers.	Any county.	7 & 8 Geo. 4, c. 53, s. 43; and 39 & 40 Vict. c. 36, s. 258.
Stealing from wrecked or stranded ships.	The county or place in which the offence was committed, or the county or place next adjoining thereto.	24 & 25 Vict. c. 96, s. 64.

CHAPTER XI.

ARTICLE 88.

THE HIGH COURT A COURT OF OYER AND TERMINER.

THE High Court of Justice (Queen's Bench Division) is a Court of Oyer and Terminer for the county of Middlesex, or for such other county as for the time being it may act in, and may as such inquire of, hear, and determine all such offences as are committed in Middlesex or such other county, or such offences by colonial governors, persons holding office in India, and others as are hereinbefore mentioned.

ARTICLE 89.

THE WRIT OF CERTIORARI.

[1] The writ of *certiorari* is a writ whereby the High Court of Justice (Queen's Bench Division) may order any proceedings to be removed from any inferior Court, and to be determined before itself or otherwise. Such writ is issued in relation to criminal proceedings in the manner and for the purposes hereinafter mentioned.

---

[1] These sections represent the effect of a good deal of legislation. At common law the writ of *certiorari* was grantable to prosecutors as of right, and to defendants at the discretion of the Court. These rights being used vexatiously, conditions were put upon them by a series of statutes, the effect of which is given in the text. The Acts are 21 Jac. 1, c. 8; 5 & 6 W. & M. c. 11; 8 & 9 W. 3, c. 33; 5 Geo. 2, c. 19; 13 Geo. 2, c. 18; 5 & 6 W. 4, c. 83; 12 & 13 Vict. cc. 45, 57; 16 Vict. c. 30. As to the origin of the writ, see 1 Hist. Cr. Law, 95.

ARTICLE 90.

WRIT WHEN DEMANDABLE BY ATTORNEY-GENERAL.

The Attorney-General acting on behalf of the Crown may as of right demand a writ of *certiorari* for the removal into the High Court of Justice (Queen's Bench Division) of any indictment or inquisition in order to its being tried before the said Court, either at bar or at *nisi prius.*

ARTICLE 91.

CONDITIONS UNDER WHICH PROSECUTOR OR DEFENDANT MAY OBTAIN CERTIORARI.

[1] The prosecutor of any indictment, and the person charged or intended to be charged by any indictment or inquisition, may move the Queen's Bench Division of the High Court or any judge of the High Court for a writ of *certiorari* to remove into that Court any indictment or presentment from any other Court.

The person making such motion or asking such leave must make it appear to the Court or judge that a fair and impartial trial of the case cannot be had in the Court below, or that some question of law of more than usual difficulty and importance is likely to arise upon the trial, or that a view of the premises in respect whereof any indictment is preferred or [[2] in cases of misdemeanor] a special jury may be required for the satisfactory trial of the same.

No *certiorari* to remove any indictment into the High Court of Justice (Queen's Bench Division) can be granted unless the party by whom it is obtained enters into recognizances, if he is prosecutor, to pay on the defendant's acquittal the costs of the defendant incurred subsequent to the removal of the indictment, and if he is the defendant, to pay if he is convicted

---

[1] Effect of 16 Vict. c. 30, ss. 4 & 5; 5 & 6 Will. 4, c. 33, s. 3; and 5 & 6 W. & M. c. 11, s. 2. The last two Acts are practically embodied by references in s. 5 of the first Act. The Acts contain some other provisions which it is not necessary to mention here.

[2] These words are probably implied, though they are not expressed.

the prosecutor's costs incurred subsequent to the removal of
such indictment, and also to appear and plead to the said
indictment or presentment in the said High Court, and at his
own cost to procure the issue joined upon the said indictment
or presentment or any plea relating thereto to be tried at the
next assizes to be held for the county wherein the said
indictment or presentment was found after the *certiorari* is
returnable, if not in the cities of London, Westminster, or
county of Middlesex, and if in the said cities or county then
to cause or procure it to be tried the next term after the
certiorari is granted, or the sittings after the term, or at such
time as the Court shall appoint.

ARTICLE 92.

CERTIORARI ISSUED BY CENTRAL CRIMINAL COURT.

[1] The High Court (Queen's Bench Division) or any judge
thereof, or any judge of the High Court of Justice being a
commissioner of oyer and terminer for the Central Criminal
Court, or the Recorder for the City of London, may on the
conditions stated in Article 91 issue a writ of *certiorari* to her
Majesty's justices of the peace for the cities of London and
Westminster, the liberty of the Tower of London, the borough
of Southwark, the counties of Middlesex, Essex, Kent, and
Surrey, or either of them, commanding the said justices of the
peace or any or either of them to certify and return into the
said court of oyer and terminer and gaol delivery, indictments
or presentments found or taken before the said justices of the
peace or any of them of any offences cognizable by the Central
Criminal Court Act, and the several recognizances, examinations, and depositions relative to such indictments and
presentments, so that the said offences may be dealt with, tried,
and determined by the said justices and judges of oyer and
terminer and gaol delivery ; and also for the like purpose they
may by writ of *habeas corpus* cause any person who may be
in the custody of any prison charged with any offence cog-

---

[1] 4 & 5 Will. 4, c. 36, s. 17.

nizable under the Central Criminal Court Act to be removed into the custody of the keeper of the gaol of Newgate.

ARTICLE 93.

INDICTMENTS AND INQUISITIONS REMOVED BY CERTIORARI, HOW DISPOSED OF.

When an indictment or inquisition has been removed by *certiorari* into the High Court (Queen's Bench Division) it may either

(*a.*) be tried before the High Court by a jury of the county from which it was removed, or

(*b.*) be sent by the said Court to be tried as a *nisi prius* record in the county from which it was removed, or

(*c.*)[1] be sent by the said Court to be tried at the Central Criminal Court.

ARTICLE 94.

WHAT CASES MAY BE ORDERED TO BE TRIED AT THE CENTRAL CRIMINAL COURT.

[2] The High Court (Queen's Bench Division) or any judge thereof in vacation may, if it appears to such Court or judge expedient for the ends of justice that any person committed or held to bail for any felony or misdemeanor committed or supposed to have been committed at any place out of the jurisdiction of the Central Criminal Court should be tried for such offence at such Court, order that he shall be so tried. Thereupon a writ of *certiorari* shall be issued to the justices of oyer and terminer, or of gaol delivery, or of the peace, before whom any indictment or inquisition charging such person with such offence is pending, or before whom any such indictment is thereafter found, or to the coroner before whom any inquisition is or is to be taken, commanding them to certify and return such indictment and inquisition to the Central Criminal Court.

---

[1] 19 Vict. c. 16, s. 1.

[2] 19 Vict. c. 16, s. 3. This Act is extremely elaborate, and contains a large number of subsidiary provisions, not necessary to be here inserted. See 1 Hist. Cr. Law, 260.

[1] The person charged must be tried in the Central Criminal Court in the same manner as if the offence had been committed within its jurisdiction and the indictment had been originally presented at or returned to the said Court.

ARTICLE 95.

SOLDIERS COMMITTED FOR THE HOMICIDE OF OTHER SOLDIERS.

[2] When any [3] soldier is committed for the murder or manslaughter of any other soldier at any place in England out of the jurisdiction of the Central Criminal Court, the High Court of Justice (Queen's Bench Division) or any judge thereof in vacation may, upon the application of her Majesty's principal Secretary of State for the War Department in a form prescribed by the Act, order the prisoner to be indicted and tried at the Central Criminal Court, and upon such order the murder or manslaughter of the deceased may be inquired of, heard, and determined, and the prisoner may be indicted, arraigned, tried, and convicted in the same manner in all respects as if such offence had been committed within the jurisdiction of the Central Criminal Court.

[1] 19 Vict. c. 16, s. 7.

[2] 25 & 26 Vict. c. 65. This Act also is extremely elaborate. As it is hardly ever used, I have given its effect very shortly.

[3] "Person subject to the present or any future Mutiny Act."

PART III.

ARREST, EXAMINATION BEFORE JUSTICES, AND COMMITTAL OF OFFENDERS, WITH PROCEEDINGS INCIDENTAL THERETO.

CHAPTER XII.—OF SUMMARY ARREST.

CHAPTER XIII.—PROCEEDINGS BEFORE JUSTICES — INFORMATION — SUMMONS—WARRANT.

CHAPTER XIV.— EXAMINATION BEFORE JUSTICES.

CHAPTER XV. — PROCURING EVIDENCE IN EXAMINATION BEFORE JUSTICES.

CHAPTER XVI.—BAIL AND RECOGNIZANCES.

CHAPTER XII.

[1] *OF SUMMARY ARREST.*

ARTICLE 96.

ARREST WITHOUT WARRANT.

ANY person, whether a peace-officer or not, may arrest without warrant any one

[2] who commits a felony in his presence, or

[2] who gives a dangerous wound in his presence, or

[3] whom he reasonably suspects of having committed a felony, if a felony has in fact been committed, or

[4] whom he [5] finds committing an indictable offence in the night, or

[1] 1 Hist. Cr. Law, 184, 200.

[2] 2 Hawk. c. 12, s. 1.

[3] 1 Hale, 490; Fost. 318. *Allen* v. *L. & S. W. R. Co.*, 40 L. J. (Q.B.) 55.

[4] 14 & 15 Vict. c. 19, s. 11.

[5] The words " finds committing " in this and similar Acts are to be construed strictly. *R.* v. *Phelps*, C. & M. 180 ; 1 Russ. Cr. 715.

[1] whom he finds committing an offence against the Vagrant Act, or

[2] whom he finds committing any offence against the Larceny Act, except that of angling in the daytime, or

[3] whom he finds committing any offence against the Coinage Offences Act, or

[4] who makes signals at night for the purpose of giving notice to any person on board any smuggling ship.

Persons found committing any offence against the [5] Act for the Prevention of Night Poaching may be arrested without warrant by the owner of the land trespassed upon, or his servants and their assistants.

[6] Persons found committing any offence against the Malicious Injuries to Property Act may be arrested without warrant by the owner of the property injured, or his servants or persons authorized by him.

[7] Persons found committing offences against the Police (Metropolitan) Act, 1839, or the Town Police Clauses Act, 1847, may be arrested without warrant by the owners of the property on or with regard to which the offence was committed, or their servants or persons authorized by them.

[8] Persons found illegally taking or intending to take salmon at night contrary to the Salmon Fishery Acts may be arrested by any water bailiff and his assistants.

---

[1] 5 Geo. 4, c. 83, s. 6. This Act is amended by the Prevention of Crimes Act, 1871, which provides that in order to prove an intent to commit a felony under the Vagrant Act it shall not be necessary to prove any particular act of the party charged, but the intent may be inferred from the circumstances of the case and the known character of the party charged. 34 & 35 Vict. c. 112, s. 15.

[2] 24 & 25 Vict. c. 96, s. 103.

[3] 24 & 25 Vict. c. 99, s. 31.

[4] 39 & 40 Vict. c. 36, s. 190. The section says that any person offending against it "may be arrested," without specifying by whom. Night, for the purposes of the section, means after sunset and before sunrise between the 21st of September and the 1st of April, and after 8 P.M. and before 6 A.M. during the rest of the year.

[5] 9 Geo. 4, c. 69, s. 2.

[6] 24 & 25 Vict. c. 97, s. 61.

[7] 2 & 3 Vict. c. 47, s. 16, and 10 & 11 Vict. c. 89, s. 13.

[8] 36 & 37 Vict. c. 71, s. 38, and 41 & 42 Vict. c. 39, s. 8.

ARTICLE 97.

ASSISTING PEACE-OFFICER TO ARREST.

[1] Any person who is required by a peace-officer to assist him in making an arrest is bound to give his assistance, and is while assisting under the same protection as the peace-officer.

ARTICLE 98.

ARREST WITHOUT WARRANT BY POLICE OFFICERS.

A peace-officer may arrest without warrant, in addition to the persons mentioned in the last Article,

(*a.*) [2] any person whom he suspects upon reasonable grounds of having committed a felony, whether a felony has in fact been committed or not;

(*b.*) [3] any person committing a breach of the peace in his presence; [4] the peace-officer may detain any such person while the breach of the peace continues or there is any danger of its renewal;

(*c.*) [5] any person whom he finds lying or loitering in any highway, yard, or other place during the night, and whom he has good cause to suspect of having committed or being about to commit any felony against the Larceny Act, the Malicious Injuries to Property Act, or the Offences against the Person Act;

(*d.*) [6] any person whom he finds loitering at night within the Metropolitan District, and who cannot give a satisfactory account of himself, or whom he suspects of evil designs;

(*e.*) [7] any person found committing a "street offence" against the Police (Metropolitan) Act, 1839, or the Town Police Clauses Act, 1847;

[1] 1 Hale, 461–3; *R.* v. *Porter*, 12 Cox, C. C. 444.
[2] Arch. 753; 1 Russ. Cr. 721.
[3] 2 Hale, 86; 4 Bla. Com. 289.
[4] 1 East, P. C. 305; *R.* & *M.* C. C. R. 132; *R.* v. *Light*, D. & B. C. C. 332.
[5] 24 & 25 Vict. c. 96, s. 104; c. 97, s. 57; and c. 100, s. 66.
[6] 10 Geo. 4, c. 44, s. 7.
[7] 2 & 3 Vict. c. 47, s. 54; 10 & 11 Vict. c. 89, s. 28.

(*f.*)[1] any offender against the Police (Metropolitan) Act, 1839, whose name and address he does not know, or any disorderly person whom he has good cause to suspect of having committed or being about to commit any felony, misdemeanor, or breach of the peace, or who is charged with a recent aggravated assault.

[1] 2 & 3 Vict. c. 47, ss. 63–65.

CHAPTER XIII.

[1] *PROCEEDINGS BEFORE JUSTICES—INFORMATION—*
SUMMONS—WARRANT.

ARTICLE 99.

INFORMATION.

[2] PROCEEDINGS taken before a justice or justices to compel the appearance of a person suspected of having committed an indictable offence with a view to his accusation by a grand jury must in all cases begin by an information.

Where it is intended to issue a summons in the first instance the information may be by parol merely, and need not be on oath.

[3] Where it is intended to issue a warrant in the first instance, an information and complaint thereof in writing on the oath or affirmation of the informant or of some witness or witnesses on that behalf must be laid before such justice or justices.

---

[1] For history of the preliminary inquiry see 1 Hist. Cr. Law, 216–233.

[2] 11 & 12 Vict. c. 42, s. 8. The words of this statute are extremely clumsy, but they imply what is stated in the text. It is enacted by 44 & 45 Vict. c. 60, s. 3, that "no criminal prosecution shall be commenced against any proprietor, publisher, or editor, or any person responsible for the publication of a newspaper, for any libel published therein without the written fiat or allowance of the Director of Public Prosecutions being first had and obtained." The Act is silent as to what amounts to commencing a criminal prosecution. Probably laying an information or taking out a summons would be a commencement, as the case of indictments is separately provided for.

[3] The Police (Metropolitan) Act, 1839 (2 & 3 Vict. c. 71, s. 21), seems to enable the stipendiary police magistrates for the metropolitan districts to issue warrants in the first instance upon verbal information on oath. The effect of Jervis's Act is given in the text.

ARTICLE 100.

SUMMONS.

[1] The justice or justices receiving the information may thereupon issue a summons directed to the party charged in the information. The summons must state shortly the matter of the information, and must require the party to whom it is directed to appear, at a certain time and place therein mentioned, before the justice who has issued the summons, or before such other justice or justices of the same [2] district as may then be there, to answer the charge. The summons must be served by a constable or other peace-officer upon the person to whom it is directed by delivering it to him personally, or, if he cannot conveniently be met with, by leaving it with some person for him at his last or most usual place of abode ; and the constable or peace-officer who served the same must attend at the time and place, and before the justices mentioned in the summons, to depose, if necessary, to the service of the said summons.

ARTICLE 101.

WARRANT IN DEFAULT OF APPEARANCE ON SUMMONS.

[3] If a person served with a summons does not appear at the time and place mentioned in the summons, the justice or justices may issue a warrant for apprehending the person summoned [apparently without any information except that on which the summons was granted].

ARTICLE 102.

WARRANT IN FIRST INSTANCE.

[4] If an information and complaint in writing, on the oath or affirmation of the informant, or of some witness or

---

[1] 11 & 12 Vict. c. 42, s. 9.
[2] County, riding, division, liberty, city, borough, or place.
[3] 11 & 12 Vict. c. 42, s. 9.
[4] Ibid. ss. 8, 9.

witnesses in that behalf, for any indictable offence is laid before any justice, he may issue a warrant for apprehending the person charged in the information.

' ARTICLE 103.

WARRANT, HOW ISSUED AND DIRECTED, AND CONTAINING WHAT.

[1] A warrant to apprehend any person charged with any indictable offence must be under the hand and seal of every justice issuing the same.

It may be issued either

to any constable or other person by name, or

to the constable of the parish or other district within which it is to be executed without naming him, or

to such constable and all other constables or peace-officers in the county or district within which the justice issuing the warrant has jurisdiction, or

generally to all the constables or peace-officers within such county or district.

It must state shortly the offence on which it is founded, and must name or otherwise describe the offender; and it must order the person or persons to whom it is directed to apprehend the offender, and bring him before the justice issuing the warrant, or before some other justice of the peace for the same district, to answer the charge contained in the information. It need not be made returnable at any particular time, but may remain in force until it is executed.

ARTICLE 104.

WARRANT WHERE AND BY WHOM EXECUTED WITHOUT BACKING.

[2] The warrant may be executed without being backed (as described in Articles 105, 106, 107) by apprehending the offender at any place within the [3] district where the justice issuing the

---

[1] 11 & 12 Vict. c. 42, s. 10.
[2] Ibid.
[3] *R. v. Cumpton*, 5 Q. B. D. 341.

same has jurisdiction, or in case of fresh pursuit at any place in the next adjoining county or place, and within seven miles of the border of such first-mentioned district. If the warrant is directed to all constables or other peace-officers within the county or other district within which the justice issuing the same has jurisdiction, any peace-officer for any precinct [1] within the jurisdiction for which such justice acted when he granted the warrant may execute the warrant within any precinct within the said jurisdiction as if the warrant had been directed specially to him by name.

ARTICLE 105.

BACKING ENGLISH WARRANTS IN ENGLAND.

[2] If any person against whom a warrant is issued is not found within the jurisdiction of the justice by whom the warrant was issued, or is or is supposed to be in any place in England or Wales out of the jurisdiction of the justice issuing such warrant, any justice of the peace for the county or place in which such person is or is supposed to be, upon proof alone being made on oath of the handwriting of the justice who issued the warrant, may make an indorsement on the warrant, signed with his name, authorizing the execution of the warrant within his jurisdiction. Such an indorsement is sufficient authority to the person bringing the warrant, and to all other persons to whom the warrant was originally directed, and also to all constables and other peace-officers of the county or place where the warrant is so indorsed, to execute the warrant in that county or place, and to carry the person against whom the warrant was issued before the justice of the peace who first issued it, or before some other justice of the peace for the same county or place, or for the county or place where the offence mentioned in the warrant appears therein to have been committed.

---

[1] Parish, township, hamlet, or place.
[2] 11 & 12 Vict. c. 42, s. 11.

ARTICLE 106.

BACKING ENGLISH WARRANTS IN OTHER PARTS OF THE
UNITED KINGDOM AND VICE VERSÂ.

[1] Warrants issued in England or Wales by any justice of
the peace, or judge of the Queen's Bench Division, or justice
of oyer and terminer or gaol delivery, may be indorsed in a
similar manner and with a similar effect to those mentioned in
Article 105 in Ireland, Scotland, or any of the [2] Isles of Man,
Guernsey, Jersey, Alderney, or Sark, by any justice of the
peace or officer having jurisdiction to issue warrants or processes in the nature of warrants in those parts of the United
Kingdom respectively. And warrants or processes in the
nature of warrants issued in any of those parts of the United
Kingdom may be indorsed in a similar manner and with
similar effects by justices of the peace in England or
Wales.

ARTICLE 107.

BACKING SCOTCH WARRANTS IN IRELAND AND VICE VERSÂ.

[3] Warrants issued in Scotland by the Lord Justice General,
Lord Chief Justice Clerk, or any of the Lords Commissioners
of Justiciary, or by any sheriff or steward depute or substitute or justice of the peace, or in Ireland by any justice of
the peace, or judge of the Queen's Bench Division, or justice
of oyer and terminer or gaol delivery, may be indorsed in
a similar manner and with similar effects to those mentioned
in Article 105 in Ireland and Scotland respectively.

[1] 11 & 12 Vict. c. 42, ss. 11–15.

[2] These powers may be exercised by the bailiffs of Jersey and Guernsey
respectively, or, in their respective absence, the lieutenant-bailiffs of those islands
respectively, within their respective bailiwicks and jurisdictions; the judge of
Alderney, or, in his absence, any jurat of that island, within that island; the
seneschal of Sark, or, in his absence, his deputy, within that island. 14 & 15
Vict. c. 55, s. 18.

[3] 11 & 12 Vict. c. 42, ss. 14, 15.

ARTICLE 108.

[1] NO OBJECTION TO BE TAKEN TO INFORMATION, SUMMONS,
OR WARRANT FOR ANY DEFECT OR VARIANCE.

[2] No objection can be taken or may be allowed to any information, summons, or warrant for any alleged defect therein in substance or form, or for any variance between it and the evidence adduced on the part of the prosecution before the justice or justices who take the examinations of the witnesses in that behalf; but if it appears to the justice or justices that the party charged has been deceived or misled by any such variance between the summons or warrant and the evidence adduced, he or they may at the request of the party charged adjourn the hearing of the case to some future day, and in the meantime remand the party charged or admit him to bail in the manner hereinafter mentioned.

[3] The fact that a defendant is illegally brought before the justices on a warrant issued without written information or oath does not oust the justices' jurisdiction.

---

[1] It seems that this applies only to objections at the hearing before the magistrate. It probably is not meant to apply to any effect which the illegality of a warrant might have upon the legality of an arrest under it.

[2] 11 & 12 Vict. c. 42, ss. 9, 10.

[3] *Reg. v. Hughes,* 4 Q. B. D. 614.

CHAPTER XIV.

[1] *EXAMINATION BEFORE JUSTICES.*

ARTICLE 109.

EXAMINATION.

WHEN any person charged with an offence for which justices have jurisdiction to commit him for trial appears or is brought before such justices, whether in custody or not, the justices must proceed in the following manner.

ARTICLE 110.

WITNESSES FOR PROSECUTION.

[2] The justices must in the presence of the accused person take the statement on oath or affirmation of those who know the facts and circumstances of the case. Before any such witness is examined the justices must administer to him the usual oath or affirmation which they have full power and authority to do. The accused person is at liberty to put questions to the witnesses against him, either by himself or by his [3] counsel or solicitor.

ARTICLE 111.

STATEMENT BY THE ACCUSED.

[4] After the examination of all the witnesses on the part of

---

[1] 1 Hist. Cr. Law, 216–33.

[2] This is the effect of 11 & 12 Vict. c. 42, s. 17.

[3] The right of the accused to have counsel or a solicitor acting for him at his examination is incidentally recognized by that part of s. 17 which concerns the deposition of witnesses who die, &c., before the trial. It is usual to allow counsel to address the justices on behalf of the accused, but *semble* that this is in the justices' discretion.

[4] 11 & 12 Vict. c. 42, s. 18.

the prosecution, the justices must cause to be read to the accused the depositions taken against him, and must then say to him these words, or words to the like effect:

" Having heard the evidence, do you wish to say anything in answer to the charge? You are not obliged to say anything unless you desire to do so, but whatever you say will be taken down in writing and may be given in evidence against you upon your trial."

Whatever the prisoner may say in answer thereto must be taken down in writing and read over to him and signed by the justices.

ARTICLE 112.

WITNESSES ON BEHALF OF THE ACCUSED.

[1] After the statement (if any) of the accused person the justices must ask him whether he desires to call any witness, and if he calls any witnesses the justices must in the presence of the accused take the statement on oath or affirmation, both examination and cross-examination, of the witnesses so called who know anything relating to the facts and circumstances of the case or anything tending to prove the innocence of the accused,[2] but except in the cases mentioned in the Article next following, it is not the duty of a committing magistrate to hear evidence in justification or excuse of the offence alleged to have been committed.

ARTICLE 113.

EVIDENCE IN CASES OF NEWSPAPER LIBEL.

[3] A court of summary jurisdiction, upon the hearing of a charge against a proprietor, publisher or editor, or any person

---

[1] This is the effect of 30 & 31 Vict. c. 35, s. 3. The words are "immediately after obeying the directions of the 18th section" of 11 & 12 Vict. c. 42. This section relates to the statement referred to in the last Article, but it may be doubted whether, if the evidence for the prosecution appears insufficient, the justices ought not to discharge the accused before calling upon him to make a statement. See next Article.

[2] *R.* v. *Carden,* L. R. 5 Q. B. D. 1.

[3] 44 & 45 Vict. c. 60, s. 4.

responsible for the publication of a[1] newspaper for a libel published therein, may receive evidence as to the publication being for the public benefit, and as to the matters charged in the libel being true, and as to the report being fair and accurate and published without malice, and as to any matter which under the Newspaper Libel and Registration Act or otherwise might be given in evidence by way of defence by the person charged on his trial on indictment, and the Court, if of opinion after hearing such evidence that there is strong or probable presumption that the jury on the trial would acquit the person charged, may dismiss the case.

ARTICLE 114.

OPTION OF DEFENDANT IN CERTAIN CASES OF NEWSPAPER LIBEL.

[2] If a court of summary jurisdiction, upon the hearing of any such charge as aforesaid for a libel published in a newspaper, is of opinion that, though the person charged is shown to have been guilty, the libel was of a trivial character, and that the offence may be adequately punished by virtue of the powers herein mentioned, the Court must cause the charge to be reduced into writing and read to the person charged, and then address a question to him to the following effect, " Do you desire to be tried by a jury or do you consent to the case being dealt with summarily ? " and if such person assents to the case being dealt with summarily the Court may summarily convict him, and adjudge him to pay a fine not exceeding £50.

ARTICLE 115.

DISCHARGE OR COMMITMENT OF THE ACCUSED.

[3] When all the evidence offered on the part of the prosecu-

---

[1] A newspaper is defined to be any paper containing public news or observations thereon published for sale at intervals not exceeding twenty-six days. 44 & 45 Vict. c. 60, s. 1.

[2] 44 & 45 Vict. c. 60, s. 5.

[3] 11 & 12 Vict. c. 42, s. 25. Qu.: Ought not the justices first to take his statement? Sections 18 and 25 provide that something is to be done after

tion has been heard, the justices if they are of opinion that
it is not sufficient to put the accused on his trial for any indictable offence must order him to be discharged as to the
information then under inquiry. If they are of opinion that
the evidence is sufficient to put the accused party upon his
trial for an indictable offence, or if the evidence given raises
a strong or probable presumption of the guilt of the accused,
they must by their warrant commit him to the common gaol
or house of correction for the [1] district to which by law he
may be committed, or admit him to bail as hereinafter
mentioned.

ARTICLE 116.

REMOVAL OF PRISONER TO GAOL.

[2] Upon the commitment of the accused person, the constable
or constables, or other persons to whom the warrant of commitment is directed, must convey the accused person to the
prison mentioned in the warrant, and deliver him together
with the warrant of commitment to the gaoler, keeper, or
governor of such prison.

ARTICLE 117.

REMANDS.

[3] If, from the absence of witnesses or any other reasonable
cause, it becomes necessary or advisable to defer the examination or further examination of the witnesses for any time, the
justices may by their warrant from time to time remand the
party accused for such time as by them in their discretion is
deemed reasonable, not exceeding eight clear days, to some
[4] prison or place of security in the district for which the

---

the evidence for the prosecution. It might be that the statement would lead to
his committal where the evidence was insufficient.

   [1] "County, riding, division, liberty, city, borough, or place."

   [2] 11 & 12 Vict. c. 42, s. 26.

   [3] Ibid. s. 21.

   [4] "The common gaol, or house of correction, or other prison, lock-up, house, or
place of security."

justices are then acting, or if the remand be for a time not exceeding three clear days the justices may verbally order the constable or other person in whose custody the accused is, or any other person named by them in that behalf, to keep the party accused in his custody, and to bring him before them or such other justices as may be there acting at the time appointed for continuing such examination. The justices may order the accused to be brought before them at any time when he is under remand, and the person in whose custody he is must obey such order.

ARTICLE 118.

EXAMINATION OF PERSON CHARGED WITH HAVING COMMITTED AN OFFENCE IN ANOTHER DISTRICT.

[1] Wherever a person appears or is brought before justices of the peace in the district wherein they have jurisdiction, charged with having committed an offence in any county or place within England or Wales wherein they have not jurisdiction, they must examine such witnesses and receive such evidence in proof of the charge as is produced before them within their jurisdiction, and if in their opinion such evidence is sufficient proof of the charge made against the accused party they shall thereupon commit him to the common gaol or house of correction for the district where the offence is alleged to have been committed, or admit him to bail as hereinafter mentioned, and must bind over the prosecutor (if he has appeared before them) and the witnesses by recognizances accordingly as hereinafter mentioned.

If the evidence is not in the opinion of the justices sufficient to put the accused party on his trial, they must bind over such witnesses as they have examined by recognizance to give evidence as hereinafter mentioned, and they must by warrant under their hands and seals order the accused party to be taken before some justices of the peace for the district where, and near to the place where the offence is alleged to have been committed, and must at the same time

[1] 11 & 12 Vict. c. 42, s. 22.

deliver the information and complaint, also the depositions and recognizances taken by them, to the constable who has the execution of the last-mentioned warrant, to be by him delivered to the justices before whom he takes the accused in obedience to the said warrant. The said depositions and recognizances are deemed to be taken in the case, and must be treated to all intents and purposes as if they had been taken before the last-mentioned justices.

CHAPTER XV.

COMMITMENT WITHOUT PREVIOUS PROCEEDINGS.

ARTICLE 119.

COMMITMENT FOR TRIAL FOR PERJURY BY JUDGES AND MAGISTRATES.

[1] THE judges or judge of any Division of the High Court of Justice, or of the Bankruptcy Court, or any of Her Majesty's justices or commissioners of assize, nisi prius, oyer and terminer or gaol delivery, or any justices of the peace, recorder or deputy recorder, chairman or other judge holding any general or quarter sessions of the peace, or any judge or deputy judge of any county court, or of any court of record, or any justices of the peace in special or petty sessions, or any sheriff or his lawful deputy before whom any writ of inquiry or any writ of trial from any of the superior courts is executed, may, in case it appears to him or them that any person has been guilty of wilful and corrupt perjury in any evidence given or in any affidavit, deposition, examination, answer or other proceeding made or taken before him or them, direct such person to be prosecuted for perjury, in case there appears to him or them a reasonable cause for such prosecution.

ARTICLE 120.

PERSON SO DIRECTED OR PROSECUTED TO BE COMMITTED OR BAILED.

[2] Such judge or judges or other person or persons as aforesaid may commit such person so directed to be prosecuted

---

[1] 14 & 15 Vict. c. 100, s. 19.
[2] Ibid.

until the next session of oyer and terminer or gaol delivery for the county or other district within which such perjury was committed unless such person enters into a recognizance with one or more sufficient surety or sureties conditioned for the appearance of such person at such next session of oyer and terminer or gaol delivery, and that he will then surrender and take his trial and not depart the court without leave, and may require any person he or they may think fit to enter into a recognizance conditioned to prosecute or give evidence against such person so directed to be prosecuted as aforesaid.

ARTICLE 121.

CERTIFICATE AND COSTS OF PROSECUTION.

[1] Such judge or judges or other person or persons as aforesaid may give to the party so bound to prosecute as aforesaid a certificate of the same being directed, which certificate must be given without any fee or charge, and is deemed sufficient proof of such prosecution having been directed as aforesaid. Upon the production thereof the costs of such prosecution must be allowed by the Court before which any person is prosecuted or tried in pursuance of such direction as aforesaid, unless such last-mentioned Court specially otherwise directs. No such direction or certificate may be given in evidence upon any trial to be had against any person upon a prosecution so directed as aforesaid.

[1] 14 & 15 Vict. c. 100, s. 19

CHAPTER XVI.

PROCURING EVIDENCE AT THE EXAMINATION BEFORE JUSTICES.

ARTICLE 122.

PROCURING THE ATTENDANCE OF WITNESSES—SUMMONS.

[1] IF it is made to appear to any justice of the peace by the oath or affirmation of any credible person that any person within his jurisdiction is likely to give material evidence for the prosecution [[2] upon the examination before any justices of any person charged with an indictable offence] and that he will not voluntarily appear for the purpose of being examined as a witness at the time and place appointed for such examination, such justice must issue his summons to such person under his hand and seal requiring him to appear at a time and place therein mentioned before him or such other justices for the same district as shall then be there, to testify what he knows concerning the charge made against the accused party.

ARTICLE 123.

PROCURING THE ATTENDANCE OF WITNESSES—WARRANT.

[3] If any person summoned as a witness as described in Article 122 neglects or refuses to appear at the time and place appointed by such summons, and no just excuse is offered for such neglect or refusal, then (after proof upon oath or affirmation of such summons having been served

---

[1] 11 & 12 Vict. c. 42, s. 16.

[2] The words enclosed in brackets are not in the statute, but some such words seem to be required to complete the sense.

[3] Ibid.

upon such person either personally or by leaving the same for him with some person at his last or most usual place of abode) the justice before whom such person should have appeared as aforesaid may issue a warrant under his hand and seal to bring such person at a time and place to be therein mentioned before him or such other justice or justices of the peace for the same district as may then be there, to testify what he knows concerning the charge made against the accused party. Such a warrant may if necessary be backed as described in Articles 105–107, in order to its being executed out of the jurisdiction of the justice who issued it.

A justice who is satisfied by evidence upon oath or affirmation that it is probable that any such person as is before mentioned will not attend to give evidence without being compelled to do so, may, instead of issuing a summons as aforesaid, issue a warrant in the first instance, which may be backed as aforesaid.

ARTICLE 124.

WITNESS REFUSING TO BE EXAMINED.

[1] If on the appearance of a person summoned before a justice [for the purpose of giving evidence], either in obedience to the summons or upon being brought before the justice on a warrant, such person refuses to be examined upon oath or affirmation concerning the offence alleged to have been committed, or refuses to take such oath or affirmation, or having taken such oath or affirmation refuses to answer such questions concerning the charge as are then put to him, without offering any just excuse for such refusal, any justice then present and having there jurisdiction may by warrant under his hand and seal commit him to the common gaol or house of correction for the district where he then is, there to be imprisoned for any time not exceeding seven days unless in the meantime he consents to be examined and to answer concerning the charge.

[1] 11 & 12 Vict. c. 42, s. 16.

ARTICLE 125.

DEPOSITIONS.

[1] The statements of witnesses taken as described in Articles 109 and 111 must be put into writing and read over to and signed respectively by the witnesses, and must be signed also by the justices taking them.

ARTICLE 126.

DEFENDANT ENTITLED TO COPIES OF DEPOSITIONS.

[2] At any time after all the examinations of witnesses are completed and before the first day of the assizes or sessions or other first sitting of the Court at which any person committed to prison or admitted to bail as aforesaid is to be tried, such person may require, and is entitled to have of and from the officer or person having the custody of the same, copies of the depositions on which he was committed or bailed, on payment of a reasonable sum for the same, not exceeding at the rate of three-halfpence for each folio of ninety words.

ARTICLE 127.

BINDING OVER PROSECUTOR AND WITNESSES BY RECOGNIZANCES.

[3] Any justice before whom any witness is examined as aforesaid may bind by recognizance the prosecutor and every such witness to appear at the next Court of oyer and terminer or gaol delivery or Court of general or quarter sessions of the peace at which the accused is to be tried, then and there to prosecute and give evidence (both or either), as the case may be, against the party accused.

The recognizances must particularly specify the [4] occupation of every such person entering into and acknowledging

---

[1] 11 & 12 Vict. c. 42, s. 17.
[2] Ibid. s. 27.
[3] Ibid. s. 20.
[4] " Profession, art, mystery, or trade."

the same, together with his christian and surname and the [1] place of his residence, and, if his residence be in a city, town, or borough, the name of the street and the number (if any) of the house in which he resides, and whether he is owner or tenant thereof or a lodger therein.

The recognizance being duly acknowledged by the person so entering into the same, must be signed by the justice before whom it is acknowledged, and a notice thereof signed by the said justice must at the same time be given to the person bound thereby.

ARTICLE 128.

DEPOSITIONS, RECOGNIZANCES, ETC., TO BE TRANSMITTED TO THE COURT.

[2] The several recognizances taken as described in Article 127, together with the written information (if any), the depositions, the statement of the accused, and the recognizance of bail (if any), must be delivered or caused to be delivered by the justice to [3] the proper officer of the Court in which the trial is to be had, before or at the opening of the said Court on the first day of the sitting thereof, or at such other time as the judge, recorder, or justice who is to preside in such Court at the said trial may order or appoint.

ARTICLE 129.

HOW IF A WITNESS REFUSES TO ENTER INTO RECOGNIZANCE.

[4] If any witness refuses to enter into or acknowledge a recognizance as described in Article 127, the justice may by his warrant commit him to the common gaol or house of correction for the district in which the accused party is to be tried, there to be imprisoned and safely kept until after the trial of such accused party, unless in the meantime such witness duly enters into such recognizance as aforesaid before

---

[1] "Parish, township, or place."

[2] 11 & 12 Vict. c. 42, s. 20.

[3] I.e. the clerk of assize, in the case of assizes; the clerk of the court at the Central Criminal Court; the clerk of the peace at the quarter sessions.

[4] 11 & 12 Vict. c. 42, s. 20.

some one justice of the peace for the district in which such gaol or house of correction is situate :

Provided that if afterwards, from want of sufficient evidence in that behalf or other cause, the justice before whom the accused party has been brought does not commit him or hold him to bail for the offence with which he is charged, he or some other justice for the same district may by his order in that behalf order and direct the keeper of such gaol or house of correction where such witness is in custody to discharge him from the same, and such keeper must thereupon forthwith discharge him accordingly.

ARTICLE 130.

[1] SEARCH WARRANTS.

(*a.*) [2] If any credible witness proves upon oath before a justice of the peace a reasonable cause to suspect that any person has in his possession or on his premises any property whatsoever on or with respect to which any offence punishable by virtue of the Larceny Act, 1861, has been committed, the justice may grant a warrant to search for such property as in the case of stolen goods.

(*b.*) [3] If it is made to appear by information upon oath or affirmation before a justice of the peace that there is reasonable cause to believe that any person has in his custody or possession without lawful authority 'or excuse any note or bill of [4] any bank, or any frame, mould, or implement for

---

[1] Search warrants were not known at common law, but having gradually come into use, were first permitted by statute for seizing stolen goods by 22 Geo. 3, c. 58, s. 2, which was repealed by 24 & 25 Vict. c. 101, Statute Law Revision Act of 1861, and replaced by the provisions the effect of which is stated in the text.

[2] 24 & 25 Vict. c. 96, s. 103. This statute seems to justify search warrants, though the words "as in the case of stolen goods" constitute a superfluous reference to the Common Law. Search warrants were originally of doubtful legality. In 4th Inst. 176, Coke denies it. It is affirmed by Hale, 2 P. C. 113, and recognized by Lord Camden in *Entick* v. *Carington*, 19 St. Tr. 1067, where he speaks of the practice of issuing such warrants as having " crept into the law by imperceptible practice."

[3] 24 & 25 Vict. c. 98, s. 46.

[4] "The governor and company of the bank of England or Ireland, or of any body corporate, company, or person carrying on the business of bankers."

G

making paper in imitation of the paper used for such notes or bills or any such paper, or any [1] material having thereon any [2] marks capable of producing or intended to produce the impression of any such note or bill or any part thereof, or any tool, instrument, or material used or employed or intended to be used or employed in any of the operations aforesaid, or any forged [3] document, or [4] anything used or employed or intended to be used or employed in forgery, such justice may if he thinks fit grant a warrant to search for the same. Any such thing found upon such search may be carried before any justice of the district, to be by him disposed of according to law. Everything so seized shall by order of the Court where any offender against the Forgery Act is tried, or if there is no such trial then by order of the justice of the peace, be defaced and destroyed or otherwise disposed of as such Court or justice directs.

(*c.*) [5] Where it is proved on the oath of a credible witness before any justice of the peace that there is reasonable cause to suspect that any person has been concerned in counterfeiting the Queen's current coin or any such other coin as is mentioned in the Coinage Offences Act, 1861, or has in his custody or possession any such false or counterfeit coin, or any [6] instrument or machine used or intended to be used for making or counterfeiting any such coin, or any such filings, dippings, or bullion or gold or silver in dust, solution, or otherwise, as mentioned in the said Act, any justice may by warrant under his hand cause any place whatever belonging to or under the control of any suspected person to be searched either by day or night for any of the things above mentioned. If any such thing is seized it must be carried

---

[1] "Any plate, wood, stone, or other material."

[2] "Words, forms, devices, or characters."

[3] "Security, document, or instrument whatsoever."

[4] "Any machinery, frame, mould, plate, die, seal, paper, or other matter or thing used or employed, or intended to be used or employed, in the forgery of any security, document, or instrument whatever."

[5] 24 & 25 Vict. c. 99, s. 27.

[6] "Instrument, tool, or engine whatsoever, adapted and intended for the making or counterfeiting of any such coin, or other machine used or intended to be used for," &c.

before a justice of the peace, who must cause the same to be secured for the purpose of being produced in evidence against any person who may be prosecuted for any offence against the Coinage Act. All such things, after being produced in evidence or when they are not required to be produced in evidence, must forthwith be delivered to the officers of the Mint or the solicitors of the Treasury or any person authorized by them to receive the same.

(*d.*) [1] Upon reasonable cause assigned upon oath by any person before any justice of the peace for any county or place in which any [2] explosive substance or machine is suspected to be made, kept, or carried, for the purpose of being used in committing any of the felonies mentioned in the Offences Against the Person Act, 1861, any justice may issue a warrant under his hand or seal for searching in the daytime any [3] place or receptacle in which such thing is suspected to be made, kept, or carried for such purposes as are before mentioned. Every person employed in such search is to have, in executing it and taking care of the things seized, all powers and protection [4] provided by 38 Vict. c. 17 (the Explosives Act, 1875), s. 86, for persons acting under that Act.

ARTICLE 131.

[5] DEPOSITION WHEN ADMISSIBLE AS EVIDENCE.

[6] A deposition taken as described in Articles 109 and 111 may be read as evidence at the trial of the accused person, if it is then proved by the oath or affirmation of any credible witness [[7] to the satisfaction of the judge] that the deponent

[1] 24 & 25 Vict. c. 100, s. 65.

[2] "Gunpowder, or other explosive, dangerous, or noxious substance or thing, or any machine, engine, instrument, or thing" are the words of the section. They could not possibly be wider, but the meaning intended seems to be that given in the text.

[3] "House, mill, magazine, storehouse, warehouse, shop, cellar, yard, wharf, or other place, or any carriage, waggon, cart, ship, boat, or vessel."

[4] Compare 24 & 25 Vict. c. 100, s. 65; 23 & 24 Vict. c. 129; and 38 Vict. c. 17, s. 86.

[5] See 'Digest of the Law of Evidence,' 139.

[6] 11 & 12 Vict. c. 42, s. 17.

[7] *R. v. Stephenson,* L. & C. 165.

is dead, or so ill as not to be able to travel [¹ although there
may be a prospect of his recovery, ¹ or if he is kept out of the
way by the person accused, ² or probably if he is too mad to
testify], and if also it be proved that such deposition was
taken in the presence of the person accused, and that he or
his counsel or solicitor had a full opportunity of cross-
examining the witness, and if such deposition purports to
have been signed by the justice by or before whom the
same purports to have been taken, without further proof
[³ unless it is proved that such deposition was not in fact
signed by the justice purporting to sign the same, or that
the same was not in fact taken before him, or that it was
not taken upon oath or affirmation, or that any of the other
conditions contained in the Act were not complied with].

ARTICLE 132.

TAKING EVIDENCE AFTER CONCLUSION OF EXAMINATION, AND
PERHAPS BEFORE ANY CHARGE IS MADE AGAINST A
PERSON SUSPECTED.

[⁴ If an indictable offence is supposed to have been com-

¹ *R. v. Scaife*, 17 Q. B. 773.

² Analogy of *R. v. Scaife*.

³ These words are not in the Act, but seem to be required.

⁴ 30 & 31 Vict. c. 35, s. 6. This I believe to be the meaning of this section,
which as it stands in the statute book is very obscure. The Act in which it occurs
was drawn by the late Mr. Avory, Clerk to the Central Criminal Court and Deputy-
Clerk of Assize on the south-eastern circuit, and was carried through the House of
Commons by the late Mr. Russell Gurney. This section was intended originally to
enable evidence to be taken by justices for the perpetuation of testimony when no
one had been charged with an offence, but in its passage through Parliament it was
amended, or rather altered, till it assumed its present form, which is such that
there is great difficulty in reconciling the concluding provisions with the preamble.
The preamble recites the importance of perpetuating testimony, obviously having
reference to a case in which no accusation has been made. The concluding lines
of the section provide that it must be proved to the satisfaction of the Court that
reasonable notice was served upon the person (whether prosecutor or accused)
against whom it is proposed to read the evidence, and that he had an opportunity
of cross-examination. This of course restricts the operation of the section to
cases where a charge has been made, and " where it is not practicable or per-
missible " to take the evidence under the 11 & 12 Vict. c. 42, s. 17. But the only
cases in which this can happen are cases in which the examination is over and the
accused person committed for trial or out on bail. It is theoretically possible,
however, that a man who had not been actually charged might be suspected, and

mitted, and if the examination of the witness against any person accused thereof has been completed in the manner hereinbefore described, and perhaps in cases in which a person is suspected of having committed an indictable offence, but no information has been given against him and no summons or warrant issued, and if in either case a person dangerously ill and unable to travel is believed to be able] to give material and important information relating to (such) indictable offence or to a person accused thereof, and it is desirable in the interests of truth and justice that means should be provided for perpetuating such testimony and rendering the same available in the event of the death of the person giving the same [the proceedings described in the next Article may take place].

ARTICLE 133.

STATEMENT OF WITNESS.

[1] Whenever it is made to appear to the satisfaction of any justice of the peace that any person dangerously ill and, in the opinion of some registered medical practitioner, not likely to recover from such illness is able and willing to give material information relating to any indictable offence, or relating to any person accused of any such offence, and it is not practicable for any justice to take a deposition in accordance with 11 & 12 Vict. c. 42, of the person so being ill, the said justice may take in writing the statement on oath or affirmation of such person, and the said justice must thereupon subscribe the same, and add thereto by way of caption a statement of his reason for taking the same, and of the day and place, when and where the same was taken, and of the names of the persons (if any) present at the taking thereof,

---

the words are, I think, wide enough to cover such a case, though if a magistrate were ever asked to take evidence under such circumstances, I think he ought to require the person who suggested it to lay an information and proceed in the ordinary way.

[1] 30 & 31 Vict. c. 35, s. 6.

and if the same relates to any indictable offence for which any accused person is already committed or bailed to appear for trial, must transmit the same with the said addition to the proper officer of the Court for trial at which the accused person has been committed or bailed; [1] and in all other cases he must transmit the same to the clerk of the peace for the [2] district in which he has taken the same, who must preserve the same and file it of record.

ARTICLE 134.

STATEMENT WHEN ADMISSIBLE IN EVIDENCE.

[3] A statement taken as described in Articles 132 and 133 may be read in evidence either for or against the accused [4] upon his trial, if the person who made the same is proved to be dead, or if it is proved that there is no reasonable probability that such person will ever be able to travel or to give evidence, without further proof thereof if the same purports to be signed by the justice by or before whom it purports to be taken, and if it is proved to the satisfaction of the Court that reasonable notice of the intention to take such statement has been served upon the person (whether prosecutor or accused) against whom it is proposed to be read in evidence, and that such person or his counsel or solicitor had, or might have had if he had chosen to be present, full opportunity of cross-examining the deceased person who made the same [[5] unless it is proved that any of the requisitions of the Act were not complied with].

ARTICLE 135.

PRISONER TO BE PRESENT AT STATEMENT.

[6] Whenever a prisoner in actual custody has served or re-

---

[1] Practically there can be no other case. These words should have been struck out when the section was amended.

[2] "County, division, city, or borough."

[3] 30 & 31 Vict. c. 35, s. 6.

[4] "Upon the trial of any offender or offence to which the same may relate."

[5] This seems to be required.

[6] 30 & 31 Vict. c. 35, s. 7.

ceived notice of an intention to take a statement as mentioned in Articles 132 and 133, the judge or justice by whom the prisoner was committed or the visiting justices of the prison in which he is confined may by an order in writing direct the gaoler having the custody of the prisoner to convey him to the place mentioned in the said notice for the purpose of being present at the taking of the statement; and such gaoler shall convey the prisoner accordingly, and the expenses of such conveyance shall be paid out of the funds applicable to the other expenses of the prison.

CHAPTER XVII.

[1] *BAIL AND RECOGNIZANCES.*

ARTICLE 136.

PRISONER BAILABLE BEFORE A JUDGE IN VACATION-TIME.

[2] IF any person is committed for trial for any crime unless for treason or felony plainly expressed in the warrant of commitment in the vacation-time and out of term, the person so committed or detained [being] other than a person convict or in execution, or any one in his behalf, may appeal or complain to the Lord Chancellor or Lord Keeper or [3] any Judge of the Queen's Bench Division of the High Court, who upon view of the copy of the warrant of commitment or detainer, or otherwise upon oath made that such copy was denied to be given by the person in whose custody the prisoner is detained, is authorized and required [[4] upon request made in writing by such person or any one on his behalf, attested and subscribed by two witnesses that were present at the delivery of the same] to grant an habeas corpus under the seal of the Court whereof he is then a judge, to be directed to the officer in whose custody the party so committed or detained is, [and] returnable immediately before the said judge.

When any person brings any habeas corpus [whether issued by the Court during the sittings or by a judge in vacation-time] directed to any sheriff or sheriff's gaoler,

---

[1] 1 Hist. Cr. Law, 233.

[2] 31 Car. 2, c. 2 (the Habeas Corpus Act). In term time the prisoner's right to be bailed for misdemeanor is a common law right.

[3] "The lord chancellor or lord keeper or any one of her Majesty's justices either of the one bench or the other, or the barons of the exchequer of the degree of the coif."

[4] These words are said in the Revised Statutes to be "annexed to the original Act in a separate schedule."

minister, or other person whatsoever, for any person in his custody, and the writ is served upon the officer or left at the gaol or prison with any of the under officers, the said officer must within three days after the service thereof (unless the commitment were for treason or felony plainly and specially expressed in the warrant of commitment) make return of the writ or bring, or cause to be brought, the body of the party before the Court which or judge who issued the writ, upon payment or tender by the party serving the writ of the expenses of bringing up the prisoner and upon security given by his own bond for the charges of carrying back the prisoner if the Court so directs.

[The person making the return must also] certify the true causes of the detainer or imprisonment of the party. The time for making the return is extended to ten days if the distance is from twenty to one hundred miles, and to twenty days if it is upwards of one hundred miles. The officer in whose custody the party is must within the times herein-before limited bring the prisoner before the person who issued the writ, with the return of such writ and the true causes of the commitment and detainer, and thereupon the Court or judge, within two days after the party is brought before him, must discharge the prisoner from his imprison-ment, taking his recognizances with one or more sureties for his appearance in the Queen's Bench Division of the High Court the term following, or at the next assizes, sessions, or general gaol delivery for the county or place where the com-mitment was or where the offence was committed, or in any other Court in which the offence is properly cognizable, and shall certify the writ and recognizances into the Court in which the appearance is to be made, unless it appears to such judge that the party so committed is detained upon a legal process, order, or warrant out of some Court that has juris-diction in criminal matters, or by some warrant under the hand and seal of a judge or justice of the peace [1] for an offence which by law is not bailable.

---

[1] It seems doubtful whether this requires the Court or judge to admit to bail in cases of misdemeanor in which a magistrate has discretion to refuse bail.

ARTICLE 137.

BAIL TAKEN AT THE TIME OF THE EXAMINATION.

[1] Where any person appears or is brought before a justice of the peace charged with any felony, or with [2] any of the misdemeanors mentioned in the note hereto, such justice may in his discretion admit such person to bail upon his procuring or producing such surety or sureties as in the opinion of such justice will be sufficient to insure the appearance of the accused at the time and place when and where he is to be tried; and thereupon such justice must take the recognizance of the accused person and his surety or sureties conditioned for the appearance of the accused at the time and place of trial, and that he will then surrender and take his trial and not depart the Court without leave.

Where any person is charged before any justice with any indictable misdemeanor other than those hereinbefore mentioned, such justice, after taking the examinations in writing as described in Articles 109 and 111, instead of committing him to prison for such offence must admit him to bail in manner aforesaid.

ARTICLE 138.

BAIL TAKEN AFTER COMMITMENT.

[3] Where a person charged with any indictable offence

Does it, e.g., entitle every person who is committed for an indecent assault to be bailed even if a magistrate has refused to bail him?

[1] 11 & 12 Vict. c. 42, s. 23.

[2] "(1) any assault with intent to commit felony; (2) any attempt to commit felony; (3) obtaining or attempting to obtain property by false pretences, or receiving property stolen or obtained by false pretences; (4) misdemeanor; (5) perjury or (6) subornation of perjury; (7) concealing the birth of a child by secret burying or otherwise; (8) wilful or indecent exposure of the person; (9) riot; (10) assault in pursuance of a conspiracy to raise wages; (11) assault upon a peace-officer in the execution of his duty, or upon any person acting in his aid; (12) neglect or breach of duty as a peace-officer; (13) any misdemeanor the costs of which may be allowed out of the county rate." For the misdemeanors for which costs may be allowed out of the county rate, see Article 317, p. 204.

[3] 11 & 12 Vict. c. 42, s. 23 (abridged).

[[1] such that the committing justice might in his discretion have refused bail] is committed to prison to take his trial for the same, the justice who signed the warrant for his · commitment may in his discretion admit such accused person to bail in manner aforesaid at any time afterwards and before the first day of the sitting or session at which he is to be tried or the day to which such sitting or session may be adjourned. If the committing justice is of opinion that for the offences before mentioned the accused person ought to be admitted to bail, and in the case of all other misdemeanors whether he is or is not of that opinion, he must certify on the back of the warrant of commitment his consent to such accused party being bailed, stating also the amount of bail which ought to be required, and thereupon any justice attending or being at the prison where such accused party is in custody may on production of such certificate admit him to bail in manner aforesaid ; or if it is inconvenient for the sureties to attend at the prison to join in the recognizance of bail, the committing justice may make a duplicate of such certificate as aforesaid, and upon the same being produced to any justice of the same district he may take the recognizance of the sureties in conformity with the same, and upon such recognizance being transmitted to the keeper of such prison, and produced together with the certificate on the warrant of commitment as aforesaid, to any justice attending or being at such prison, such justice may thereupon take the recognizance of the accused and order him to be discharged out of custody as to that commitment, and the justice so admitting him to bail must forthwith transmit the recognizances of bail to the committing justice, to be by him transmitted with the examinations to the proper officer.

A person committed to prison charged with an offence for which bail cannot be refused may apply to any one of the visiting justices of such prison, or any other justice of the

---

[1] See note to Article 136, p. 89. Taken as a whole, the section obviously means this, but the words are " in all cases where a person charged with any indictable offence."

same district, before the first day of the sitting or session at which he is to be tried, or the day to which such sitting or session may be adjourned, to be admitted to bail, and such justice must admit him to bail in manner aforesaid.

ARTICLE 139.

BAIL IN CASES OF TREASON.

[1] No person charged with treason may be admitted to bail except by order of one of her Majesty's Secretaries of State, or by the Queen's Bench Division of the High Court, or a judge thereof in vacation.

ARTICLE 140.

WARRANT OF DELIVERANCE.

[2] When a justice admits to bail any person who is then in any prison charged with the offence for which he is so admitted to bail, such justice shall send or cause to be lodged with the keeper of such prison a warrant of deliverance under his hand and seal requiring the said keeper to discharge the person so admitted to bail if he is detained for no other offence, and upon such warrant being delivered to or lodged with such keeper he must forthwith obey it.

---

[1] 11 & 12 Vict. c. 42, s. 23. The words are "no justice or justices of the peace shall admit any person to bail for treason, nor shall such person be admitted to bail."

[2] 11 & 12 Vict. c. 42, s. 24.

PART IV.

EXTRADITION, FOREIGN OFFENDERS, AND RETURN OF FUGITIVE CRIMINALS FROM BRITISH POSSESSIONS.

CHAPTER XVIII,—Extradition to Foreign Countries: General Principles.

CHAPTER XIX. — Procedure for Arrest and Surrender of Foreign Fugitive Criminals.

CHAPTER XX.—Indian and Colonial Fugitive Offenders.

CHAPTER XVIII.

[1] *EXTRADITION TO FOREIGN COUNTRIES: GENERAL PRINCIPLES.*

ARTICLE 141.

EXTRADITION CRIMES. DEFINITION.

[2] An extradition crime is a crime committed out of the ordinary jurisdiction of the English Criminal Courts which if committed in England would be one of the [3] following crimes at common law or by statute :—

Murder and attempt and conspiracy to murder.

Manslaughter.

Counterfeiting and altering money and uttering counterfeit or altered money.

Forgery, counterfeiting, and altering and uttering what is forged or counterfeited or altered.

Embezzlement and larceny.

Obtaining money or goods by false pretences.

---

[1] 2 Hist. Cr. Law, 65.
[2] 33 & 34 Vict. c. 52, s. 26.
[3] 33 & 34 Vict. c. 52, 1st schedule ; and 36 & 37 Vict. c. 60, schedule.

Crimes by bankrupts against bankruptcy law.

Fraud by a bailee, banker, agent, factor, trustee, or director or member or public officer of any company made criminal by any act for the time being in force.

Rape.

Abduction.

Child stealing.

Burglary and Housebreaking.

Arson.

Robbery with violence.

Threats by letter or otherwise with intent to extort.

Piracy by the law of nations.

Sinking or destroying a vessel at sea, or attempting or conspiring to do so.

Assaults on board a ship on the high seas with intent to destroy life or to do grievous bodily harm.

Revolt or conspiracy to revolt by two or more persons on board a ship on the high seas against the authority of the master.

[1] Kidnapping and false imprisonment.

[1] Perjury and subornation of perjury whether under common or statute law.

[1] Any indictable offence not hereinbefore mentioned under the Larceny Act, 1861, the Malicious Injuries to Property Act, 1861, the Forgery Act, 1861, the Coinage Offences Act, 1861, the Offences Against the Person Act, 1861, or any Act amending or substituted for the same or any of them respectively.

[1] Any indictable offence not hereinbefore mentioned under the laws for the time being in force in relation to bankruptcy.

[2] Counselling, procuring, commanding, aiding or abetting the commission of any extradition crime, or being accessory before or after the fact to any extradition crime.

[1] 36 & 37 Vict. c. 60, schedule.
[2] Ibid. s. 3.

ARTICLE 142.

FUGITIVE CRIMINALS : DEFINITION.

[1] A fugitive criminal is any person accused or convicted of an extradition crime committed within the jurisdiction of any [2] foreign state who is in or is suspected of being in some part of Her Majesty's dominions. A fugitive criminal of a foreign state is a fugitive criminal accused or convicted of an extradition crime committed within the jurisdiction of that state.

ARTICLE 143.

RESTRICTIONS UPON SURRENDER OF FUGITIVE CRIMINALS.

[3] No fugitive criminal may be surrendered to a foreign state—

1. if, the offence in respect of which his surrender is demanded is one of a political character, or if he proves to the satisfaction of the police magistrate or of the Court before whom he is brought on *habeas corpus*, or to the Secretary of State, that the requisition for his surrender has in fact been made with a view to try or punish him for an offence of a political character :

2. No fugitive criminal shall be surrendered to any foreign state unless provision is made by the law of that state or by arrangement that the fugitive criminal shall not, until he has been restored or had an opportunity of returning to Her Majesty's dominions, be detained or tried in that foreign state for any offence committed prior to his surrender other than the extradition crime proved by the facts on which the surrender is grounded.

3. No fugitive criminal who has been accused of some offence within English jurisdiction not being the offence for which his surrender is asked, or who is undergoing sentence under any conviction in the United Kingdom, may be

[1] 33 & 34 Vict. c. 52, s. 26.
[2] These words include every colony, dependency, and constituent part of a foreign state, and every vessel of that state. 33 & 34 Vict. c. 52, s. 25.
[3] 33 & 34 Vict. c. 52, s. 3.

surrendered until after he has been discharged whether by acquittal or on expiration of his sentence or otherwise:

4. No fugitive criminal may be surrendered until after the expiration of fifteen days from the date of his being committed to prison to await his surrender.

ARTICLE 144.

ORDERS IN COUNCIL.

[1] Where an arrangement has been made with any foreign state with respect to the surrender to such state of any fugitive criminals Her Majesty may by Order in Council direct that the Extradition Acts, 1870, 1873, shall apply in the case of such foreign state.

Her Majesty may by the same or any subsequent Order limit the operation of the Order, and restrict the same to fugitive criminals who are in or suspected of being in the part of Her Majesty's dominions specified in the Order, and render the operation thereof subject to such conditions, exceptions, and qualifications as may be deemed expedient.

Every such Order must recite or embody the terms of the arrangement and must not remain in force for any longer period than the arrangement.

Every such Order must be laid before both Houses of Parliament within six weeks after it is made, or if Parliament be not then sitting, within six weeks after the then next meeting of Parliament, and must also be published in the *London Gazette*.

[2] Such Order must not be made unless the arrangement:—

1. Provides for the determination of it by either party after the expiration of a notice not exceeding one year: and

2. Is in conformity with the provisions of the Extradition Acts, 1870, 1873, and in particular with the [3] restrictions on the surrender of fugitive criminals contained in those Acts.

---

[1] 33 & 34 Vict. c. 52, s. 2.
[2] Ibid. s. 4.
[3] See Article 143.

ARTICLE 145.

PUBLICATION AND EFFECT OF ORDER.

[1] When an Order applying the said Acts in the case of any foreign state has been published in the *London Gazette*, the said Acts (after the date specified in the Order, or if no date is specified, after the date of the publication) apply in the case of such foreign state so long as the Order remains in force, but subject to the limitations, restrictions, conditions, exceptions and qualifications, if any, contained in the Order.

An Order in Council is conclusive evidence that the arrangement therein referred to complies with the requisitions of the said Act, and that the said Act applies in the case of the foreign state mentioned in the Order. The validity of such Order cannot be questioned in any legal proceedings whatever.

ARTICLE 146.

APPLICATION OF THE ACTS.

[2] Where the said Acts apply in the the case of any foreign state, every fugitive criminal of that state who is in or suspected of being in any part of Her Majesty's dominions, or that part which is specified in the Order applying the Acts (as the case may be), may be apprehended and surrendered in the manner hereinafter mentioned at [3] whatever time the crime in respect of which the surrender sought is committed, and whether there is or is not any concurrent jurisdiction in any Court of Her Majesty's dominions over that crime.

[1] 33 & 34 Vict. c. 52, s. 5.
[2] Ibid. s. 6.
[3] This is the effect of 36 & 37 Vict. c. 60, s. 2.

CHAPTER XIX.

PROCEDURE FOR ARREST AND SURRENDER OF FOREIGN FUGITIVE CRIMINALS.

ARTICLE 147.

REQUISITION FOR SURRENDER OF FUGITIVE CRIMINALS.

[1] A REQUISITION for the surrender of a fugitive criminal of any foreign state who is in or suspected of being in the United Kingdom must be made to a Secretary of State by some person recognized by the Secretary of State as a diplomatic representative of that foreign state.

[2] The expression diplomatic representative includes any person recognized by the Secretary of State as a consul-general of that state.

ARTICLE 148.

ORDER FOR ARREST OF FUGITVE CRIMINALS.

[3] A Secretary of State may by order under his hand and seal signify to any [4] one of the Bow Street police magistrates that such requisition has been made, and require him to issue his warrant for the apprehension of such criminal.

If the Secretary of State is of opinion that the offence is one of a political character, he may, if he think fit, refuse to send any such order, and he may also at any time order a fugitive criminal accused or convicted of such an offence to be discharged from custody.

---

[1] 33 & 34 Vict. c. 52, s. 7.

[2] 36 & 37 Vict. c. 60, s. 7.

[3] 33 & 34 Vict. c. 52, s. 7.

[4] The expression "police magistrate" in the Extradition Acts means a chief magistrate of the Metropolitan Police Courts, or one of the other magistrates of the Metropolitan Police Court at Bow Street.

ARTICLE 149.

APPREHENSION OF FUGITIVE CRIMINAL.

[1] A warrant for the apprehension of a fugitive criminal, whether accused or convicted of crime, who is in or suspected of being in the United Kingdom may be issued :—

1. By a police magistrate at Bow Street on receipt of an order of the Secretary of State (see Article), and on such evidence as would in his opinion justify the issue of the warrant if the crime had been committed or the criminal convicted in England. And

2. By a police magistrate at Bow Street or any justice of the peace in any part of the United Kingdom on such information or complaint and on such evidence or after such proceedings as would in the opinion of the person issuing the warrant justify the issue of a warrant if the crime had been committed or the criminal convicted in that part of the United Kingdom in which he exercises jurisdiction.

Any person so issuing a warrant without an order from a Secretary of State must forthwith send a report of the fact of such issue, together with the evidence and information or complaint or certified copies thereof, to a Secretary of State, who may, if he think fit, order the warrant to be cancelled and the person who has been apprehended on the warrant to be discharged.

ARTICLE 150.

EXECUTION OF WARRANT OF POLICE MAGISTRATE.

[2] The warrant of the police magistrate at Bow Street may be executed in any part of the United Kingdom in the same manner as if the same had been originally issued or subsequently indorsed by a justice of the peace having jurisdiction in the place where the same is executed.

---

[1] 33 & 34 Vict. c. 52, s. 8.
[2] Ibid. s. 13.

H 2

ARTICLE 151.

FUGITIVE CRIMINAL APPREHENDED WITHOUT SECRETARY OF STATE'S ORDER.

[1] A fugitive criminal when apprehended on a warrant issued without the order of a Secretary of State must be brought before a justice of the peace,[2] who must by warrant order him to be brought, and the prisoner must accordingly be brought, before a police magistrate at Bow Street. Such prisoner must be discharged by the police magistrate at Bow Street unless such magistrate, within such reasonable time as with reference to the circumstances of the case he may fix receives from the Secretary of State an order signifying that a requisition has been made for the surrender of such criminal.

ARTICLE 152.

HEARING OF CASE BEFORE MAGISTRATE.

[3] When a fugitive criminal is brought before the police magistrate at Bow Street, such magistrate must hear the case in the same manner and has the same jurisdiction and powers as near as may be as if the prisoner were brought before him charged with an indictable offence committed in England.

ARTICLE 153.

EVIDENCE ON BEHALF OF FUGITIVE CRIMINAL.

[4] The police magistrate at Bow Street must receive any evidence which may be tendered to show that the crime of which the prisoner is accused, is :—

an offence of a political character: or

not an extradition crime.

---

[1] 33 & 34 Vict. c. 52, s. 8.

[2] Some person having power to issue a warrant under 33 & 34 Vict. c. 52, s. 8 (Article 149).

[3] 33 & 34 Vict. c 52, s. 9.

Ibid.

ARTICLE 154.

COMMITTAL OR DISCHARGE OF FUGITIVE CRIMINAL.

[1] In the case of a fugitive criminal accused of an extradition crime, if the foreign warrant authorizing such arrest is duly authenticated and such evidence is produced as (subject to the provisions of the Extradition Acts, 1870 and 1873) would, according to the law of England, justify the committal for trial of the prisoner if the crime of which he is accused had been committed in England: and in the case of a fugitive criminal alleged to have been convicted of an extradition crime if such evidence is produced as (subject to the provisions of the said Acts) would, according to the law of England prove that the prisoner was convicted of such crime:

the police magistrate at Bow Street must commit him to the Middlesex House of Detention, or to some other prison in Middlesex, there to await the warrant of a Secretary of State for his surrender;

but otherwise must order him to be discharged.

ARTICLE 155.

PROCEEDINGS UPON COMMITTAL OF FUGITIVE CRIMINAL.

If the police magistrate at Bow Street commits a fugitive criminal to prison he must:

[2] forthwith send to a Secretary of State a certificate of his committal and such report upon the case as he may think fit: and

[3] inform such criminal that he will not be surrendered until after the expiration of fifteen days, and that he has a right to apply for a writ of *habeas corpus.*

ARTICLE 156.

WARRANT FOR SURRENDER OF FUGITIVE CRIMINAL.

[4] A Secretary of State may, upon the expiration of fifteen

[1] 33 & 34 Vict. c. 52, s. 10.
[2] Ibid.
[3] Ibid. s. 11.
[4] Ibid.

days after the committal of a fugitive criminal to prison, or if a writ of *habeas corpus* is issued after the decision of the Court upon the return to the writ, as the case may be, or after such further period as [1] he thinks proper, by warrant under his hand and seal, order the fugitive criminal (if not delivered on the decision of the Court) to be surrendered to such person as may in his opinion be duly authorized to receive the fugitive criminal by the foreign state from which the requisition for the surrender proceeded; and such fugitive criminal must be surrendered accordingly.

ARTICLE 157.

EXECUTION OF WARRANT FOR SURRENDER.

[2] Any person to whom the Secretary of State's warrant is directed, and the person authorized as aforesaid, may receive, hold in custody, and convey within the jurisdiction of the foreign state the criminal mentioned in the warrant.

If such criminal escapes out of any custody to which he may be delivered on or in pursuance of such warrant, he may be retaken in the same manner as any person accused of any crime against the laws of that part of Her Majesty's dominions to which he escapes may be retaken upon an escape.

ARTICLE 158.

IF PRISONER NOT SURRENDERED WITHIN TWO MONTHS OF COMMITTAL.

[3] If a fugitive criminal who has been committed to prison is not surrendered and conveyed out of the United Kingdom within two months after such committal, or if a writ of *habeas corpus* is issued after the decision of the Court upon the return to the writ, a [4] judge of the High Court of Justice may, upon application made to him by or on behalf of the criminal, and upon proof that reasonable notice of the

---

[1] May be allowed in either case by a Secretary of State.

[2] 33 & 34 Vict. c. 52, s. 11.

[3] Ibid. s. 12.

[4] For any judge of one of Her Majesty's Superior Courts at Westminster.

intention to make such application has been given to a Secretary of State, order the criminal to be discharged out of custody unless sufficient cause is shown to the contrary.

ARTICLE 159.

FOREIGN DEPOSITIONS, &C.

[1] Depositions or statements on oath or [2] affirmation taken in a foreign state, and copies of such original depositions or statements :

and foreign certificates of or judicial documents stating the fact of conviction may,

if duly authenticated, be received in evidence in proceedings under the Extradition Acts, 1870, 1873.

ARTICLE 160.

FOREIGN WARRANTS, DEPOSITIONS, &C., HOW AUTHENTICATED.

[3] Foreign warrants and such depositions, statements, copies, certificates, or judicial documents as aforesaid, are deemed to be duly authenticated for the purposes of the Extradition Acts, 1870 and 1873, if authenticated in manner provided for the time being by law—or authenticated as follows :—

1. If the warrant purports to be signed by a judge, magistrate, or officer of the foreign state where the same was issued :

2. If the depositions or statements or the copies thereof purport to be certified under the hand of a judge, magistrate, or officer of the foreign state where the same were taken to be the original depositions or statements or to be true copies thereof, as the case may require, and

3. If the certificate of or judicial document stating the fact of conviction purports to be certified by a judge, magistrate, or officer of the foreign state where the conviction took place : and

if in every case the warrants, depositions, statements, copies,

[1] 33 & 34 Vict. c. 52, s. 14.
[2] 36 & 37 Vict. c. 60, s. 4,
[3] 33 & 34 Vict. c. 52, s. 15.

certificates and judicial documents (as the case may be) are authenticated by the oath of some witness, or by being sealed with the official seal of the Minister of Justice or some other minister of state. All courts of justice, justices and magistrates, must take judicial notice of such official seal, and must admit the documents so authenticated by it to be received in evidence without further proof.

ARTICLE 161.

CRIMES COMMITTED AT SEA.

[1] Where the crime in respect of which the surrender of a fugitive criminal is sought was committed on board any vessel on the high seas which comes into any port of the United Kingdom :—

1. Any stipendiary magistrate in England or Ireland and any sheriff or sheriff substitute in Scotland may exercise the powers and jurisdiction conferred by the Extradition Acts, 1870, 1873, upon a police magistrate at Bow Street, except so far as regards the execution of the warrant of the police magistrate. This jurisdiction is in addition to and not in derogation or exclusion of that of the police magistrate at Bow Street :

2. The criminal may be committed to any prison to which the person committing him has power to commit persons accused of the like crime :

3. If the fugitive criminal is apprehended on a warrant issued without the order of a Secretary of State he must be brought before the stipendiary magistrate, sheriff or sheriff substitute who issued the warrant or who has jurisdiction in the port where the vessel lies or in the place nearest to that port.

ARTICLE 162.

POWER OF FOREIGN STATE TO OBTAIN EVIDENCE IN UNITED KINGDOM.

[2] The testimony of any witness may be obtained in relation

---

[1] 33 & 34 Vict. c. 52, s. 16.
[2] Ibid. s. 24.

to any criminal matter provided it is not of a political character pending in any court or tribunal in a foreign state in like manner as it may be obtained in relation to any civil matter under 19 & 20 Vict. c. 113.

[1] A Secretary of State may by order under his hand and seal require a police magistrate at Bow Street or a justice of the peace to take evidence for the purposes of any criminal matter not of a political character pending in any court or tribunal in any foreign state; and such police magistrate or justice of the peace upon receipt of such order must take the evidence of every witness appearing before him for the purpose in like manner as if such witness appeared on a charge against some defendant for an indictable offence, and must certify at the foot of the depositions so taken that such evidence was taken before him, and must transmit the same to the Secretary of State. Such evidence may be taken in the presence or absence of the person charged, if any, and the fact of such presence or absence must be stated in such deposition.

Any person may, after payment or tender to him of a reasonable sum for his costs and expenses in this behalf, be compelled for the purposes of 36 & 37 Vict. c. 60, s. 5, to attend and give evidence, and answer questions and produce documents in like manner and subject to the like conditions as he may in the case of a charge preferred for an indictable offence.

ARTICLE 163.

CRIMINALS SURRENDERED BY FOREIGN STATE.

[2] Where in pursuance of any arrangement with a foreign state any person accused or convicted of any extradition crime is surrendered by that foreign state, such person cannot, until he has been restored or had an opportunity of returning to such foreign state, be triable or tried for any offence committed prior to the surrender in any part of Her Majesty's dominions other than such of the said crimes as may be proved by the facts on which the surrender is grounded.

---

[1] 36 & 37 Vict. c. 60, s. 5.
[2] 33 & 34 Vict. c. 52, s. 19.

CHAPTER XX.

˙ *INDIAN AND COLONIAL FUGITIVE OFFENDERS.* ˙

ARTICLE 164.

WHAT INDIAN AND COLONIAL FUGITIVE OFFENDERS MAY BE RETURNED.

[1] Where a person accused of having committed in one part of Her Majesty's dominions [2] any offence, however described, punishable in the part of Her Majesty's dominions in which it is committed by imprisonment with hard labour or with labour or rigorous imprisonment for twelve months or upwards, or by any greater punishment, has left that part, such person, if found in another part of Her Majesty's dominions, is liable to be apprehended and returned to the part from which he is a fugitive,[3] whether the offence of which he is accused is or is not an offence in the part of Her Majesty's dominions where he is apprehended, and whether, if it is an offence there, it is or is not such an offence [there] as is hereinbefore described.

[4] The United Kingdom, the Channel Islands, and the Isle of Man are one part of Her Majesty's dominions within the meaning of this chapter.

[5] All territories and places within Her Majesty's dominions which are under one legislature are, within the meaning of this chapter, one British possession and one part of Her Majesty's dominions.

A fugitive may be so apprehended under an endorsed warrant or a provisional warrant.

---

[1] 44 & 45 Vict. c. 69, s. 1.
[2] Effect of s. 9, which says that the Act shall apply to " treason, piracy, and to every offence whether called felony, misdemeanor, crime, or by any other name."
[3] Effect of latter part of s. 9.
[4] Effect of s. 37.
[5] Effect of s. 39. Definition of " British possession."

ARTICLE 165.

ENDORSING WARRANT.

[1] Where a warrant has been issued in one part of Her Majesty's dominions for the apprehension of a fugitive from that part, any of the following authorities in another part of Her Majesty's dominions in or on the way to which the fugitive is or is suspected to be [[2] may endorse the warrant as hereinafter mentioned] ; (that is to say,)

(1.) A Judge of a [3] Superior Court in such [last-mentioned] part ; and

(2.) In the United Kingdom a [4] Secretary of State and one of the magistrates of the Metropolitan Police Court in Bow Street ; and

(3.) In a British possession the [5] governor of that possession. [The person who endorses the warrant must before doing so be] satisfied that the warrant was issued by some person having lawful authority to issue the same. The warrant so endorsed is a sufficient authority to apprehend the fugitive in the part of Her Majesty's dominions in which it is endorsed, and bring him before a magistrate.

[6] The endorsement must authorize the persons to whom the warrant was originally directed, and any persons who

---

[1] 44 & 45 Vict. c. 69, s. 3.

[2] These words are in the original, but they are so far off from the nominative case that I have put them in here for clearness.

By s. 39 this expression means—

In England, the Court of Appeal and the High Court of Justice :

In Scotland, the High Court of Justiciary :

In Ireland, the Court of Appeal and the High Court of Justice at Dublin :

In a British possession any Court having in that possession the like criminal jurisdiction to that which is vested in the High Court of Justice in England, or such court or judge as may be determined by any act or ordinance of that possession.

[4] One of Her Majesty's principal Secretaries of State, s. 39.

[5] Any person or persons administrating the government of a British possession, including the governor and lieutenant-governor of any part of India, s. 39. Does this include a chief commissioner in India ?

[6] S. 26. I have put in a few full stops and nominative cases which seem to be wanted. Why should this section be separated from the principal one by twenty-two sections and described as a " supplemental provision " ?

are named in the endorsement and every constable, to execute the warrant within the part of her Majesty's dominions
in which the endorsement is made. The warrant is to be
executed by apprehending the person named in it, and bringing him before some magistrate in the said part, whether the
magistrate named in the endorsement or some other. The
word constable means out of England any policeman or
officer having the like power or duties.

ARTICLE 166.

PROVISIONAL WARRANT FOR APPREHENSION OF FUGITIVE.

[1] A [2] magistrate of any part of Her Majesty's dominions may
issue a provisional warrant for the apprehension of a fugitive
who is or is suspected of being in or on his way to that part on
such information, and under such circumstances, as would in
his opinion justify the issue of a warrant if the offence of
which the fugitive is accused had been committed within his
jurisdiction, and such warrant may be backed and executed
accordingly.

A magistrate issuing a provisional warrant must forthwith
send a report of the issue, together with the information or a
certified copy thereof, if he is in the United Kingdom, to a
Secretary of State, and if he is in a British possession, to the
governor of that possession, and the Secretary of State or
governor may, if he think fit, discharge the person apprehended under such warrant.

ARTICLE 167.

WHEN FUGITIVE APPREHENDED.

[3] A fugitive when apprehended must be brought before a
magistrate, who (subject to the provisions of the Fugitive

---

[1] 44 & 45 Vict. c. 69, s. 4.

[2] Except in Scotland, any justice of the peace; in Scotland a sheriff or sheriff
substitute; in the Channel Islands, the Isle of Man, or a British possession, any
person having authority for the apprehension of persons committing offences, and
to commit such persons for trial. S. 39.

[3] 44 & 45 Vict. c. 69, s. 2.

Offenders Act, 1881) must hear the case in the same manner and have the same jurisdiction and powers, as near as may be (including the power to remand and admit to bail), as if the fugitive were charged with an offence committed within his jurisdiction.

If the endorsed warrant for the apprehension of the fugitive is duly authenticated, and such evidence is produced as (subject to the provisions of the said Act) according to the law ordinarily administered by the magistrate, raises a strong or probable presumption that the fugitive committed the offence mentioned in the warrant, and that the offence is one of those above mentioned, the magistrate must commit the fugitive to prison to await his return, and must forthwith send a certificate of the committal and such report of the case as he may think fit, if in the United Kingdom to a Secretary of State, and if in a British possession to the governor of that possession.

Where the magistrate commits the fugitive to prison he must inform the fugitive that he will not be surrendered until after the expiration of fifteen days, and that he has a right to apply for a writ of *habeas corpus*, or other like process.

A fugitive apprehended on a provisional warrant may be from time to time remanded for such reasonable time not exceeding seven days at any one time, as under the circumstances seems requisite for the production of an endorsed warrant.

ARTICLE 168.

RETURN OF FUGITIVE BY WARRANT.

[1] Upon the expiration of fifteen days after a fugitive has been committed to prison to await his return, or if a writ of *habeas corpus* or other like process is issued with reference to such fugitive by a Superior Court, after the final decision of the Court in the case,

> (1.) If the fugitive is so committed in the United Kingdom, a Secretary of State; and

[1] 44 & 45 Vict. c. 69, s. 6.

(2.) If the fugitive is so committed in a British possession,
  the governor of that possession,

may, if he thinks it just, by warrant under his hand order
that fugitive to be returned to the part of Her Majesty's
dominions from which he is a fugitive, and for that purpose
to be delivered into the custody of the persons to whom the
warrant is addressed, or some one or more of them, and to be
held in custody, and conveyed by sea or otherwise to the said
part of Her Majesty's dominions, to be dealt with there in due
course of law as if he had been there apprehended, and such
warrant shall be forthwith executed according to the tenor
thereof.

The governor or other chief officer of any prison, on request
of any person having the custody of a fugitive under any such
warrant, and on payment or tender of a reasonable amount
for expenses, must receive such fugitive and detain him for
such reasonable time as may be requested by the said person
for the purpose of the proper execution of the warrant.

ARTICLE 169.

IF PERSON APPREHENDED NOT RETURNED WITHIN ONE MONTH.

[1] If a fugitive who, in pursuance of the provisions mentioned in the last Article, has been committed to prison in
any part of Her Majesty's dominions to await his return, is
not conveyed out of that part within one month after such
committal, a Superior Court, upon application by or on behalf
of the fugitive, and upon proof that reasonable notice of the
intention to make such application has been given, if the said
part is the United Kingdom to a Secretary of State, and if the
said part is a British possession to the governor of the
possession, may, unless sufficient cause is shown to the
contrary, order the fugitive to be discharged out of custody.

[1] 44 & 45 Vict. c. 69, s. 7.

ARTICLE 170.

SENDING BACK OF PERSONS NOT PROSECUTED OR ACQUITTED.

[1] Where a person accused of an offence and returned in pursuance of this part of this Act to any part of Her Majesty's dominions, either is not prosecuted for the said offence within six months after his arrival in that part, or is acquitted of the said offence, then if that part is the United Kingdom a Secretary of State, and if that part is a British possession the governor of that possession, may, if he think fit, on the request of such person, cause him to be sent back free of cost and with as little delay as possible to the part of Her Majesty's dominions in or on his way to which he was apprehended.

ARTICLE 171.

WHERE THE CASE IS FRIVOLOUS OR THE RETURN UNJUST.

[2] Where it is made to appear to a Superior Court that by reason of the trivial nature of the case, or by reason of the application for the return of a fugitive not being made in good faith in the interests of justice or otherwise, it would, having regard to the distance, to the facilities for communication, and to all the circumstances of the case, be unjust or oppressive or too severe a punishment to return the fugitive either at all or until the expiration of a certain period, such Court may discharge the fugitive, either absolutely or on bail, or order that he shall not be returned until after the expiration of the period named in the order, or may make such other order in the premises as to the Court seems just.

ARTICLE 172.

POWER OF LORD LIEUTENANT IN IRELAND.

[3] In Ireland the Lord Lieutenant or Lords Justices or other chief governor or governors of Ireland, also the chief secretary

---

[1] 44 & 45 Vict. c. 69, s. 8.
[2] Ibid. s. 10.
[3] Ibid. s. 11.

of such Lord Lieutenant, may, as well as a Secretary of State, execute any portion of the powers by the provisions mentioned in Articles 165–170 vested in a Secretary of State.

ARTICLE 173.

TRIAL OF OFFENCE OF FALSE SWEARING.

[1] A person accused of the offence (under whatever name it is known) of swearing or making any false [2] deposition, or of giving or fabricating any false evidence, for the purposes of the Fugitive Offenders Act, 1881, may be tried either in the part of Her Majesty's dominions in which such deposition or evidence is used, or in the part in which the same was sworn, made, given, or fabricated, as the justice of the case may require.

ARTICLE 174.

WARRANTS, ETC. NOT AFFECTED BY DEATH OF PERSON BY WHOM THEY ARE ISSUED.

[3] For the purposes of the said Act every warrant, summons, subpœna, and process, and every endorsement made in pursuance of the said Act thereon, remains in force, notwithstanding that the person signing the warrant on such endorsement dies or ceases to hold office.

ARTICLE 175.

ESCAPE OF PRISONER FROM CUSTODY.

[4] If a prisoner escape, by breach of prison or otherwise, out of the custody of a person acting under a warrant issued or endorsed in pursuance of the Fugitive Offenders Act, 1881, he may be retaken in the same manner as a person accused of a crime against the law of that part of Her Majesty's dominions to which he escapes may be retaken upon an escape.

---

[1] 44 & 45 Vict. c. 69, s. 22.
[2] This expression includes any affidavit, affirmation, or declaration in the case of persons allowed by law to declare or affirm without swearing.
[3] 44 & 45 Vict. c. 69, s. 26.
[4] Ibid. s. 28.

A person guilty of the offence of escaping or of attempting
to escape, or of aiding or attempting to aid a prisoner to
escape, by breach of prison or otherwise, from custody under
any warrant issued or endorsed in pursuance of the said Act,
may be tried in any of the following parts of Her Majesty's
dominions, namely, the part to which and the part from which
the prisoner is being removed, and the part in which the
prisoner escapes, and the part in which the offender is found.

ARTICLE 176.

DEPOSITIONS AND AUTHENTICATION.

[1] A magistrate may take depositions for the purposes of the
Fugitive Offenders Act, 1881, in the absence of a person
accused of an offence, in like manner as he might take the
same if such person were present and accused of the offence
before him.

Depositions (whether taken in the absence of the fugitive
or otherwise) and copies thereof, and official certificates of or
judicial documents stating facts, may, if duly authenticated,
be received in evidence in proceedings under the said Act.

Nothing in the said Act authorises the reception of any
such depositions, copies, certificates, or documents in evidence
against a person upon his trial for an offence.

Warrants and depositions, and copies thereof, and official
certificates of or judicial documents stating facts, are deemed
duly authenticated for the purposes of the said Act if they
are authenticated in manner provided for the time being by
law, or if they purport to be signed by or authenticated by
the signature of a judge, magistrate, or officer of the part
of Her Majesty's dominions in which the same are issued,
taken, or made, and are authenticated either by the oath of
some witness, or by being sealed with the official seal of a
Secretary of State, or with the public seal of a British possession, or with the official seal of a governor of a British
possession, or of a colonial secretary, or of some secretary or

[1] 44 & 45 Vict. c. 69, s. 29,

I

minister administering a department of the government of a British possession.

All courts and magistrates must take judicial notice of every such seal as is in this Article mentioned, and must admit in evidence without further proof the documents authenticated by it.

ARTICLE 177.

EXERCISE OF JURISDICTION BY MAGISTRATES.

[1] The jurisdiction under Part One of the Fugitive Offenders Act, 1881, to hear a case and commit a fugitive to prison to await his return may be exercised,—

(1.) In England, by a chief magistrate of the metropolitan police courts or one of the other magistrates of the metropolitan police court at Bow Street; and

(2.) In Scotland, by the sheriff or sheriff substitute of the county of Edinburgh; and

(3.) In Ireland, by one of the police magistrates of the Dublin metropolitan police district; and

(4.) In a British possession, by any judge, justice of the peace, or other officer having the like jurisdiction as one of the magistrates of the metropolitan police court in Bow Street, or by such other court, judge, or magistrate as may be from time to time provided by an Act or ordinance passed by the legislature of that possession.

If a fugitive is apprehended and brought before a magistrate who has no power to exercise the jurisdiction under the said Act in respect of that fugitive, that magistrate must order the fugitive to be brought before some magistrate having that jurisdiction, and such order must be obeyed.

ARTICLE 178.

ORDERS IN COUNCIL.

[2] Her Majesty in Council may from time to time make

---

[1] 44 & 45 Vict. c. 69, s. 30.
[2] Ibid. s. 31.

Orders for the purposes of the Fugitive Offenders Act, 1881, and may revoke and vary any Order so made, and every Order so made while it is in force has the same effect as if it were enacted in the said Act.

An Order in Council made for the purposes of the said Act must be laid before Parliament as soon as may be after it is made if Parliament is then in session, or if not, as soon as may be after the commencement of the then next session of Parliament.

ARTICLE 179.

OFFENCES AT SEA OR TRIABLE IN SEVERAL PARTS
OF HER MAJESTY'S DOMINIONS.

[1] Where a person accused of an offence can, by reason of the nature of the offence, or of the place in which it was committed, or otherwise, be, under the Fugitive Offenders Act, 1881, or otherwise, tried for or in respect of the offence in more than one part of Her Majesty's dominions, a warrant for the apprehension of such person may be issued in any part of Her Majesty's dominions in which he can, if he happens to be there, be tried; and each part of the said Act applies, as if the offence had been committed in the part of Her Majesty's dominions where such warrant is issued, and such person may be apprehended and returned in pursuance of the said Act, notwithstanding that in the place in which he is apprehended a court has jurisdiction to try him:

Provided that if such person is apprehended in the United Kingdom a Secretary of State, and if he is apprehended in a British possession, the governor of such possession, may, if satisfied that, having regard to the place where the witnesses for the prosecution and for the defence are to be found, and to all the circumstances of the case, it would be conducive to the interests of justice so to do, order such person to be tried in the part of Her Majesty's dominions in which he is apprehended, and in such case any warrant previously issued for his return shall not be executed.

[1] 44 & 45 Vict. c. 69, s. 33.

I 2 .

ARTICLE 180.

CONVICTS.

[1] Where a person convicted by a court in any part of Her Majesty's dominions of an offence committed either in Her Majesty's dominions or elsewhere, is unlawfully at large before the expiration of his sentence, each part of the Fugitive Offenders Act, 1881, applies to such person, so far as is consistent with the tenor thereof, in like manner as it applies to a person accused of the like offence committed in the part of Her Majesty's dominions in which such person was convicted.

ARTICLE 181.

REMOVAL OF PERSON TRIABLE IN MORE THAN ONE PART OF HER MAJESTY'S DOMINIONS.

[2] Where a person accused of an offence is in custody in some part of Her Majesty's dominions, and the offence is one for or in respect of which, by reason of the nature thereof or of the place in which it was committed or otherwise, a person may under the Fugitive Offenders Act, 1881, or otherwise be tried in some other part of Her Majesty's dominions, in such case a superior court, and also if such person is in the United Kingdom a Secretary of State, and if he is in a British possession the governor of that possession, if satisfied that, having regard to the place where the witnesses for the prosecution and for the defence are to be found, and to all the circumstances of the case, it would be conducive to the interests of justice so to do, may by warrant direct the removal of such offender to some other part of Her Majesty's dominions in which he can be tried, and the offender may be returned, and, if not prosecuted or acquitted, sent back free of cost in like manner as if he were a fugitive returned in pursuance of Part One of the said Act, and the warrant were a warrant for the return of such fugitive, and the provisions of the said Act shall apply accordingly.

---

[1] 44 & 45 Vict. c. 69, s. 34.
[2] Ibid. s. 5.

ARTICLE 182.

FOREIGN JURISDICTION.

[1] Her Majesty may from time to time by Order in Council direct that the Fugitive Offenders Act, 1881, shall apply as if, subject to the conditions, exceptions, and qualifications (if any) contained in the Order, any place out of Her Majesty's dominions in which Her Majesty has jurisdiction, and which is named in the Order, were a British possession, and may provide for carrying into effect such application.

ARTICLE 183.

CHANNEL ISLANDS AND ISLE OF MAN.

[2] The Fugitive Offenders Act, 1881, extends to the Channel Islands and Isle of Man as if they were part of England and of the United Kingdom, and the United Kingdom and those islands are deemed for the purpose of the said Act to be one part of Her Majesty's dominions; and a warrant endorsed in pursuance of Part One of the said Act may be executed in every place in the United Kingdom and the said islands accordingly.

ARTICLE 184.

PAST OFFENCES.

The Fugitive Offenders Act, 1881, applies to offences committed before the commencement of the said Act, (1st January, 1882) in like manner as if such offence had been committed after such commencement.

---

[1] 44 & 45 Vict. c. 69, s. 36.
[2] Ibid. s. 37.

PART V.

ACCUSATION.

CHAPTER XXI.

[1] *ACCUSATION BY AN INDICTMENT.*

ARTICLE 185.

OF INDICTMENTS.

[2] AN indictment is a written accusation of one or more persons of a crime preferred to and presented upon oath by a grand jury; but the grand jury may if they please present an indictment upon their own knowledge.

---

[1] 1 Hist. Cr. Law, 273-294. It is said that in some cases a verdict in a civil action may operate as an indictment, but if this was ever true it is obsolete. See 2 Hawk. P. C. ch. 52, s. 6. Lord Ellenborough (*R.* v. *Johnson*, 29 St. Tr. 400) said he had heard of such cases, but had never known of one.

[2] Archb. 1; and see 2 Hale, P. C. 153. The word presentment is also used. It is a more general term than indictment, including, e.g., a coroner's inquisition.

CHAPTER XXII.

OF PREFERRING AN INDICTMENT BEFORE A GRAND JURY.

ARTICLE 186.

[1] OF THE GRAND JURY.

WHENEVER any Court is to sit for the trial of indictable offences, a grand jury must be summoned for the purpose of receiving such indictments as may be preferred before them.

The grand jury must consist of not less than twelve, and not more than twenty-three persons, and an indictment may by any number not less than twelve.

ARTICLE 187.

QUALIFICATION OF GRAND JURORS.

[2] It seems that no qualification at all is required for grand jurors for the Assizes, either by statute or at common law.

In practice the grand jury at the Assizes consists of county magistrates, a list of whom is called over at the opening of the Courts in order that they may appear.

[3] The following persons are qualified and liable to serve on grand juries in courts of sessions of the peace in the county, riding, or division in which they respectively reside :—

(*a.*) Every man (except certain exempted persons) between the ages of twenty-one and sixty years, residing in any county in England, who has in his own name or in trust for him

---

[1] For the history of Grand Juries see 1 Hist. Cr. Law, 250–272.

[2] It is said in Archbold that no qualification is required (p. 82), but that the grand jurors must be "of the king's liege people, of whom none shall be outlawed," &c. (11 Hen. 4, c. 9), but this Act is repealed by 26 & 27 Vict. c. 125, the Repealing Act, 1863.

[3] 6 Geo. 4, c. 50, s. 1.

within the same county, ten pounds by the year above reprizes in lands or tenements, whether of freehold, copyhold or customary tenure, or of ancient demesne, or in rents issuing out of any such lands or tenements, or in such lands, tenements, or rents taken together, in fee simple, fee tail, or for the life of himself or some other person, or

(*b.*) who has within the same county twenty pounds by the year above reprizes in lands or tenements held by lease or leases for the absolute term of twenty-one years, or some longer term or for any term of years determinable on any life or lives, or

(*c.*) who being a householder is rated or assessed to the poor-rate or to the inhabited house duty in the county of Middlesex on a value of not less than £30, or in any other county on a value of not less than £20, or

(*d.*) who occupies a house containing not less than fifteen windows.

ARTICLE 188.

PROCEDURE BEFORE THE GRAND JURY.

Indictments drawn in the manner and according to the rules hereinafter specified are taken before the grand jury by the solicitors for the prosecution of the persons indicted.

ARTICLE 189.

SWEARING WITNESSES BEFORE GRAND JURY.

[1] The foreman of the grand jury, or any member thereof for the time being acting on behalf of such foreman in the examination of witnesses in support of any bill of indictment, is authorized and required to administer an oath or affirmation to all persons whomsoever who appear before such grand jury to give evidence in support of any bill of indictment, and all such persons attending before any grand jury to give evidence may be sworn, or affirm, and examined upon oath or affirmation by such grand jury touching the matters

---

[1] 19 & 20 Vict. c. 54. It is provided that taking a false oath before the grand jury shall be perjury.

in question. The name of every witness examined or intended to be so examined must be indorsed on such bill of indictment, and the foreman of such grand jury must write his initials against the name of each witness so sworn or affirming, and examined touching such bill of indictment.

It is not necessary for any person to take an oath in open court in order to qualify such person to give evidence before any grand jury.

ARTICLE 190.

EXAMINATION OF WITNESSES—FINDING BILLS.

The grand jury examine, or if they see fit allow the solicitor for the prosecution to examine, the witnesses whose names are indorsed on the back of the indictment, or so many of them as they think proper. As soon as they are satisfied that a *primâ facie* case is made out against the person accused, they return a true bill against him, in which case the foreman indorses upon the indictment the words "a true bill." If they think that there is no such case made out, they return no true bill, in which case the foreman indorses upon the indictment the words "no true bill." In every case the foreman signs the indorsement.

True bills so indorsed are brought by the grand jury into the court, and handed by the foreman to the clerk of the court.

ARTICLE 191.

RIGHT TO PRESENT BILLS.

Any person may present a bill to any grand jury accusing any other person whatever of any crime whatever, without giving any previous notice to such person, and without taking any previous preceedings before any justice or coroner, except in the cases specified in the next Article.

ARTICLE 192.

VEXATIOUS INDICTMENT ACTS.

[1] No bill of indictment for any of the offences hereinafter

[1] 22 & 23 Vict. c. 17, s. 1.

specified may, [1] without the consent of the Court in or before which the same is preferred, be presented to or found by any grand jury,

unless the prosecutor or other person presenting such indictment has been bound by recognizance to prosecute or give evidence against the person accused of such offence, or

unless the person accused has been committed to or detained in custody or has been bound by recognizance to appear to answer to an indictment to be preferred against him for such offence, or

unless such indictment for such offence if charged to have been committed in England is preferred by the direction or with the consent in writing of a judge of one of the superior Courts of Law at Westminster, or of her Majesty's Attorney-General or Solicitor-General for England, or in the case of an indictment for perjury by the direction of any Court, judge, or public functionary authorized by 14 & 15 Vict. c. 100, to direct a prosecution for perjury.

The said offences are : Perjury, subornation of perjury, conspiracy, obtaining money or other property by false pretences, keeping a gambling house, keeping a disorderly house, any indecent assault,[2] libel, and any offence under the Newspaper Libel and Registration Act, 1881.

ARTICLE 193.

WHEN COUNTS MAY BE ADDED.

[3] The presentment to or finding by a grand jury of any bill of indictment containing a count or counts for any of the said offences is not unlawful if such count or counts be such as might on the 1st of October, 1867, be lawfully joined with the rest of such bill of indictment; and if the same count or counts are founded (in the opinion of the Court in or before which the same bill of indictment is preferred) upon the facts or evidence disclosed in any examinations or depositions

---

[1] 30 & 31 Vict. c. 35, s. 1.
[2] 44 & 45 Vict. c. 60, s. 6
[3] 30 & 31 Vict. c. 35, s. 1.

taken before a justice of the peace in the presence of the person accused or proposed to be accused by such bill of indictment and transmitted or delivered to such Court in due course of law.

ARTICLE 194.

BINDING OVER TO PROSECUTE WHERE MAGISTRATE REFUSES TO COMMIT.

[1] Where any charge or complaint is made before any justice of the peace that any person has committed any of the said offences within the jurisdiction of such justice, and such justice refuses to commit or to bail the person charged with such offence to be tried for the same, then in case the prosecutor desires to prefer an indictment respecting the said offence, the said justice must take the recognizance of such prosecutor to prosecute the said charge or complaint, and transmit such recognizance, information, and depositions (if any) to the Court in which such indictment ought to be preferred in the same manner as he would have done if he had committed the person charged to be tried for such offence.

ARTICLE 195.

PROCESS TO COMPEL APPEARANCE ON INDICTMENT—BENCH WARRANT.

[2] If an indictment is found against a person who is neither in custody nor on bail, or who being under recognizance to appear and answer any indictment that may be preferred against him does not so appear, the person who prosecutes the indictment may apply to the Court for a Bench Warrant, and if such a warrant is issued the person mentioned in it may be arrested in any part of England, and conveyed to the prison for the district in which the Court sits, there to be detained till he is tried or bailed.

[3] A bench warrant must be applied for and granted while the Court is sitting.

[1] 22 & 23 Vict. c. 17, s. 2.
[2] Archb. 88.
[3] Archb. 88 ; 2 Hawk. ch. 27, s. 8.

If it is granted at the assizes or at the Central Criminal Court it is signed by a judge; if at the sessions by two justices of the peace.

ARTICLE 196.

PROCESS TO COMPEL APPEARANCE ON INDICTMENT—CERTIFICATE.

[1] Where any indictment is found in any court of oyer and terminer or general gaol delivery or sessions of the peace against any person who is then at large, whether such person has been bound by any recognizance to appear to answer to the same or not, the person who acts as clerk of indictments or clerk of the peace at such court at which the said indictment is found must, at any time afterwards after the end of the sessions of oyer and terminer or gaol delivery or sessions of the peace at which such indictment has been found, upon application of the prosecutor, or of any person on his behalf, and on payment of a fee of one shilling, if such person has not already appeared and pleaded to such indictment, grant unto such prosecutor or person a certificate of such indictment having been found. Upon production of such certificate to any justice of the peace for any district in which the offence is in the indictment alleged to have been · committed, or in which the person indicted in and by such indictment resides or is or is supposed or suspected to reside or be, such justice must issue his warrant to apprehend such person so indicted, and to cause him to be brought before him or any other justice for the same district to be dealt with according to law.

If such person is apprehended and brought before any such justice, such justice upon its being proved upon oath or affirmation before him that the person so apprehended is the same person who is charged and named in such indictment must without further inquiry or examination commit him for trial or admit him to bail.

If such person so indicted is confined in any gaol or prison for any other offence than that charged in the said indictment at the time of such application and production of the said certificate to such justices as aforesaid, such justice must, upon it being proved before him upon oath or affirmation that the person so indicted and the person so confined in prison are one and the same person, issue his warrant directed to the gaoler or keeper of the gaol or prison in which the person so indicted is then confined as aforesaid, commanding him to detain such person in his custody until by Her Majesty's writ of *habeas corpus* he is removed therefrom for the purpose of being tried upon the said indictment or until he is otherwise removed or discharged out of the custody by due course of law.

CHAPTER XXIII.

[1] *CRIMINAL INFORMATION AND PROCESS THEREON.*

ARTICLE 197.

CRIMINAL INFORMATION.

A CRIMINAL information is an accusation made either by the Attorney-General or the Solicitor-General or by the Master of the Crown Office.

ARTICLE 198.

CRIMINAL INFORMATION BY ATTORNEY- OR SOLICITOR-GENERAL.

The Attorney-General or the Solicitor-General may without sending an indictment before a grand jury file a criminal information against any person accusing him of any misdemeanor. Informations are usually filed in cases of misdemeanors having a tendency to disturb the public peace or to interfere with good government, as for instance, cases of seditious libel or other libels in which the public are interested, cases of official corruption or fraud or misconduct, cases of bribery.

An information is filed by being deposited in a place appointed for that purpose in the Crown Office, to which place the public have the right of access at proper times. When such an information is so filed the Master of the Crown Office [2] may give notice thereof to the person against whom it is filed.

ARTICLE 199.

APPEARANCE.

The defendant may at any time after the filing of the in-

---

[1] For history of Criminal Informations see 1 Hist. Cr. Law, 294–7.

[2] This is now a common practice, but the Attorney-General can if he pleases proceed at once under Article 201.

formation appear and plead or demur to the information. This is done by an entry in a book kept for that purpose in the Crown Office, which entry may be made either in person or by the defendant's solicitor.

ARTICLE 200.

DEFENDANT IN QUEEN'S BENCH DIVISION MUST PLEAD IN FOUR DAYS.

[1] Where any person is prosecuted in the Queen's Bench Division for any misdemeanor, either by information or by indictment there found or removed into the same, and appears in term time in the said Court in person to answer to such indictment or information, such defendant upon being charged therewith [[2] is not permitted to imparle to a following term but] is required to plead or demur thereto within four days from the time of his appearance, and in default of his pleading or demurring within four days as aforesaid, judgment may be entered against the defendant for want of a plea.

In case such defendant appears to such indictment or information by his clerk or solicitor in Court, such defendant may not imparle to a following term, but a rule requiring such defendant to plead may forthwith be given, and a plea or demurrer to such indictment or information enforced, or judgment by default entered thereupon, in the same manner as might have been done before the passing of 60 Geo. 3 & 1 Geo. 4. c. 4 (23 December, 1819), in cases where the defendant had appeared to such indictment or information by his clerk in Court or attorney in a previous term.

But the said Division or a judge thereof may upon sufficient cause shown for that purpose allow further time for such defendant to plead or demur to such indictment or information.

[1] 60 Geo. 3 & 1 Geo. 4, c. 4, ss. 1 & 2.
[2] Imparlances are now at an end, but the words are kept as being in the Act.

ARTICLE 201.

PROCEDURE IN DEFAULT OF APPEARANCE—-HOLDING TO
BAIL ON JUDGE'S WARRANT.

[1] Where any person is charged with any misdemeanor for
which he may be prosecuted by indictment or information in
the Queen's Bench Division and the same is made to appear
to any judge of the same Division by affidavit or by certificate
of an indictment or information being filed against such
person in the said Court for such misdemeanor, such judge
may issue his warrant under his hand and seal and thereby
cause such person to be apprehended and brought before
him or some other judge of the same Division, or before some
justice of the peace, in order to his being bound to the
Queen's Majesty with two sufficient sureties in such sum as
in the said warrant is expressed with condition to appear in
the said Division at the time mentioned in such warrant, and
to answer all and singular indictments or informations for
any such offence.

In case any such person neglects or refuses to become
bound as aforesaid, such judge or justice respectively may
commit such person to the common gaol of the county,
city, or place where the offence was committed or where
he was apprehended, there to remain until he has become
bound as aforesaid or is discharged by order of the said Division during the sittings, or of one of the judges of the said
Division in vacation.

The recognizance thereupon taken must be returned and
filed in the said Division, and continues in force until such
person has been acquitted of such offence, or in case of conviction has received judgment for the same, unless sooner
ordered by the said Division to be discharged.

[1] 48 Geo. 3, c. 58, s. 1.

ARTICLE 202.

IF PERSON COMMITTED ON JUDGE'S WARRANT REFUSES TO APPEAR AND PLEAD.

[1] Where any person, either by virtue of such warrant of commitment as aforesaid or by virtue of any [2] writ of *capias ad respondendum* issued out of the said Division, is committed to and detained in any gaol for want of bail, the prosecutor of such indictment or information may cause a copy thereof to be delivered to such person, or to the gaoler, keeper, or turnkey of the gaol wherein such person is so detained, with a notice thereon indorsed that unless such person, within eight days from the time of such delivery of a copy of the indictment or information, causes an appearance and also a plea or demurrer to be entered in the said Division to such indictment or information, an appearance and the plea of not guilty will be entered thereto in the name of such person.

In case he thereupon for the space of eight days after such delivery of a copy of the indictment or information neglects to cause an appearance and also a plea or demurrer to be entered in the said Division to such indictment or information, the prosecutor, upon an affidavit (taken before any judge of the High Court or any commissioner authorized to take affidavits) being made and filed in the said Division of the delivery of a copy of such indictment or information with such notice indorsed thereon as aforesaid to such person or to such gaoler, keeper, or turnkey, as the case may be, may cause an appearance and the plea of not guilty to be entered in the said Division to such indictment or information for such person. Such proceedings must be had thereupon as if the defendant had appeared and pleaded not guilty according to the usual course of the said Division.

[1] 48 Geo. 3, c. 58, s. 1.
[2] See Article on Outlawry.

K

ARTICLE 203.

A COPY OF ATTORNEY-GENERAL'S INFORMATION TO BE DELIVERED.

[1] Where the Attorney- or Solicitor-General has instituted a prosecution for misdemeanor in the Queen's Bench Division, either by information or indictment, not found or removed into the said Division, the Court must if required make order that a copy of the information or indictment shall be delivered, after appearance, to the party prosecuted, or his clerk in Court, or attorney, upon application made for the same, free from all expense to the party so applying, provided that such party, or his clerk in Court, or attorney, has not previously received a copy thereof.

ARTICLE 204.

WHEN INFORMATION BY THE ATTORNEY-GENERAL IS NOT BROUGHT TO TRIAL WITHIN TWELVE MONTHS.

[2] Where any prosecution for a misdemeanor instituted by the Attorney- or Solicitor-General in the Queen's Bench Division is not brought to trial within twelve calendar months next after the plea of not guilty has been pleaded therein, the Court, upon application made on the behalf of any defendant in such prosecution, of which application twenty days' previous notice must be given to the Attorney- or Solicitor-General, may make an order, if the said Court sees just cause to do so, authorizing such defendant to bring on the trial in such prosecution, and the defendant may bring on such trial accordingly, unless a *nolle prosequi* has been entered in such prosecution.

ARTICLE 205.

CRIMINAL INFORMATION BY MASTER OF CROWN OFFICE.

[3] The Master of the Crown Office in the Queen's Bench

---

[1] 60 Geo. 3 & 1 Geo. 4, c. 4, s. 8.
[2] Ibid. s. 9.
[3] 4 W. & M. c. 18, s. 1.

Division may not exhibit, receive, or file any information for any misdemeanor without express order given by the said Division in open Court.

ARTICLE 206.

IN WHAT CASES A RULE FOR A CRIMINAL INFORMATION IS GRANTED.

[1] A rule for a criminal information to be issued by the Master of the Crown Office at the instance of a private prosecutor may be granted for any misdemeanor, but it is usually granted in the following and in similar cases only:

libels on private individuals attended with circumstances of aggravation;

illegal acts committed by magistrates or inferior public officers from corrupt or vindictive motives, and not merely from ignorance or mistake.

The Court does not in general grant a criminal information against any person for an illegal act committed by him under a *bonâ fide* conviction that he was exercising a legal right.

No application may be made for an information against a magistrate for anything done in execution of his office unless previous notice of the application has been given to him. The application must be made within a reasonable time after the commission of the offence, [2] except [perhaps] in the case of bribery in parliamentary elections.

The application for an information must be made upon an affidavit disclosing all the facts of the case.

ARTICLE 207.

PROCEDURE WHEN A RULE FOR A CRIMINAL INFORMATION IS GRANTED.

[3] When the Master of the Crown Office in the Queen's Bench Division has exhibited, received, or filed any informa-

---

[1] Archb. 118–122.
[2] Archb. 121; *R.* v. *Heming*, 5 B. & Ad. 666.
[3] 4 W. & M. c. 18, s. 2.

tion by leave of the Court as aforesaid, he may not issue out any process upon any such information before he has taken or has had delivered to him a recognizance from the person procuring such information to be exhibited, with the place of his abode, title, or profession, to be entered to the person against whom such information is to be exhibited, in the penalty of twenty pounds, that he will effectually prosecute such information, and abide by and observe such orders as the said Court directs. The said recognizance may be taken by the said Master of the Crown Office or by any justice of the peace of the district where the cause of such information arises.

The Master of the Crown Office after he has taken such recognizance or received it from any justice must make an entry thereof upon record, and file a memorandum thereof in some public place in his office, that all persons may resort thereunto without fee.

The Queen's Bench Division may award to the defendant his costs:

if the defendant appears to the information and pleads to issue, and the prosecutor of such information does not at his own proper costs and charges within one whole year next after issue joined therein procure the same to be tried:

or if upon such trial a verdict passes for the defendant:

or if the informer procures a *nolle prosequi* to be entered:

unless the judge before whom the information is tried certifies upon record at such trial in open Court that there was a reasonable cause for exhibiting such information.

If upon such award the informer does not within three months next after the costs are taxed pay the said costs to the defendant, the defendant has the benefit of the said recognizance to compel him thereunto.

ARTICLE 208.

DISCHARGE OF PERSON ACQUITTED.

[1] If upon the trial of such indictment or information any

---

[1] 48 Geo. 3, c. 58, s. 1.

defendant so committed and detained as aforesaid is acquitted
of all the offences therein charged upon him, the judge
before whom such trial is had may order that such defendant
shall be forthwith discharged out of custody as to his commitment as aforesaid, and such defendant must be thereupon
discharged accordingly.

CHAPTER XXIV.

ACCUSATION BY A CORONER'S INQUEST.

ARTICLE 209.

THE OFFICE OF THE CORONER.

[1] " A coroner of our lord the king ought to inquire of these things : first when coroners are commanded by the king's bailiffs or by honest men of the country, they shall go to the places where any be slain, or suddenly dead, or wounded, or where [2] houses are broken, or where treasure is said to be found, and shall forthwith command four of the next towns, or five or six, to appear before him in such a place, and when they are come thither the coroner upon the oath of them shall inquire." [3]

[1] 4 Edw. 1, st. 2, ss. 1, 2 (*De Officio Coronatoris*, 1276).

[2] This is obsolete in practice. For a case of an inquest for treasure trove, see *R. v. Thomas*, L. & C. 313.

[3] The nature of the inquiry is given in the statute. The provisions are obsolete, but are curious. They are as follows :—" If it concerns a man slain, whether they know where the person was slain, whether it were in any house, field, bed, tavern, or company, and if any and who were there. Likewise it is to be inquired who were and in what manner culpable either of the act or of the force, and who were present, either men or women, and of what age soever they be (if they can speak, or have any discretion). And how many soever be found culpable by inquisition in any of the manners aforesaid, they shall be taken and delivered to the sheriff and committed to the gaol, and such as shall be founden and be not culpable shall be attached until the coming of the justices, and their names shall be written in the rolls of the coroners. If it fortune any such man be slain in the fields or woods and be there found, first it is to be inquired whether he were slain there or not, and if he were brought and laid there they shall do so much as they can to follow their steps that brought the body thither, or of the horse which brought him, or cart, if perchance he was brought upon a horse or cart. It shall be inquired also if the dead person were known or else a stranger, and where he lay the night before. In like manner it is to be inquired of them that be drowned or suddenly dead, and after it is to be seen of such bodies whether they are so drowned or slain or strangled by the sign of a

ARTICLE 210.

WHEN INQUESTS ARE TO BE HELD AND ON WHOSE INFORMATION.

[1] It is the duty of the coroner having jurisdiction in the place to which any prison [subject to the Prisons Acts of 1865 & 1877] belongs to hold an inquest on the body of every prisoner who may die within [any such] prison. Where it is practicable, one clear day must intervene between the day of the death and the day of holding the inquest.

[2] It is at common law the duty of the coroner of the district to hold an inquest on the body of every prisoner who dies in any prison whatever, and it is the duty of every gaoler of every prison to give the coroner notice of every such death.

[3] When any person is executed within a prison under the provisions of the "Capital Punishment Amendment Act 1868" (31 Vict. c. 24), the coroner of the jurisdiction to which the prison belongs must within twenty-four hours after the execution hold an inquest on the body of the offender, and the jury at the inquest must inquire into and ascertain the identity of the body and whether judgment of death was duly executed on the offender, and the inquisition must be in duplicate, and one of the originals must be delivered to the sheriff. No officer of the prison, or prisoner confined therein, may in any case be a juror on the inquest.

---

cord tied strait about their necks, or about any of their members, or upon any other hurt found upon their bodies, whereupon they shall proceed in the form abovesaid. And if they were not slain, then ought the coroner to attach the finders and all others in the company. A coroner ought also to inquire of all treasure that is found who know the finders, and likewise who is suspected thereof, and that may be well perceived where one liveth riotously, haunting taverns, and hath done so of long time. Hereupon he may be attached for this suspicion by four or six or more pledges if they may be found." The rest of the statute concerns appeals.

[1] 28 & 29 Vict. c. 126, s. 48.

[2] 3 Inst.; 2 Hawk. P. C. 79; Jervis, 30. The Prisons Act of 1865 (28 & 29 Vict. c. 126) does not apply to prisons for convicts under the directors of convict prisons or to any military or naval prisons. The common law will apply to such cases, unless there is some special provision to the contrary in special Acts relating to them.

[3] 31 Vict. c. 24, s. 5.

[1] In case of the death of any insane person in any hospital or licensed house or asylum, or under the care of any person as a single patient, a statement setting forth the time and cause of the death and the duration of the disease of which such patient died must be prepared and signed by the medical person who attended the patient during the illness which terminated in death, and such statement must be entered in the " Case Book," and a copy of such statement, certified by the superintendent or proprietor, must within two days of the date of the death be transmitted to the coroner for the county or borough, and in case such coroner after receiving such statement thinks that any reasonable suspicion attends the cause and circumstances of the death of such patient he must summon a jury to inquire into the cause of such death.

[2] When an infant dies in a house registered for the receiving of infants for the purpose of nursing them for hire, under the Infant Life Protection Act (35 & 36 Vict. c. 38) the person registered must, within twenty-four hours after the death of such infant, cause notice thereof to be given to the coroner for the district, and the said coroner must hold an inquest on the body of every such infant, unless a certificate under the hand of a registered medical practitioner is produced to him by the person so registered, certifying that such registered medical practitioner has personally attended or examined such infant, and specifying the cause of its death, and the said coroner is satisfied by such certificate that there is no ground for holding such inquest.

[3] In other cases it is the duty of the coroner to hold an inquest if he has a reasonable ground of suspicion that any

---

[1] 16 & 17 Vict. c. 96, s. 19, and 25 & 26 Vict. c. 111, s. 44.

[2] 35 & 36 Vict. c. 38, s. 8.

[3] Jervis, 30a. Inquests held upon the bodies of persons killed in explosions or idents in mines to which the Coal Mines Regulation Act, 1872, or the Metalliferous Mines Regulation Act, 1872, apply, or on a railway or by any injury received on a railway, or by any explosion of any explosive or any accident connected therewith, are subject to certain statutory regulations as to returns by the coroner, the presence of inspectors, who may serve on the jury, &c. 35 & 36 Vict. c. 76, s. 50; 35 & 36 Vict. c. 77, s. 22; 36 & 37 Vict. c. 76, s. 5; 38 Vict. c. 17, s. 65.

person has come to his death by violent and unnatural means, or that he has died suddenly from some unknown cause; but if he hears only that some person has died, however suddenly, by some known and natural cause, it is his duty not to hold an inquest or to make inquiries likely to be painful to the feelings of the family of the person deceased.

ARTICLE 211.

LOCAL JURISDICTION OF CORONERS.

[1] The coroner within whose jurisdiction the body of any person upon whose death an inquest ought to be holden is lying dead must hold the inquest notwithstanding that the cause of death did not arise within the jurisdiction of such coroner; and in the case of any body found dead in the sea, or any creek, river, or navigable canal within the flowing of the sea, where there is no deputy-coroner for the jurisdiction of the Admiralty of England, the inquest must be holden only by the coroner having jurisdiction in the place where the body is first brought to land.

[2] For the purpose of holding coroners' inquests, every detached part of a [3] district is deemed to be within that district by which it is wholly surrounded, or where it is partly surrounded by two or more districts, within that one with which it has the longest common boundary.

[4] If a verdict of murder or manslaughter, or as accessory before the fact to any murder, is found by the jury at any such inquest against any person, the coroner holding the said inquest has the same powers for the commitment of the person so charged as they possessed by law previously to the passing of the Act 6 Vict. c. 12 (11 April, 1843), with regard to the commitment of any person committed within the jurisdiction where the death happened.

[1] 6 Vict. c. 12, s. 1.
[2] Ibid. s. 2.
[3] " County, riding, or division."
[4] 6 Vict. c. 12, s. 3.

CHAPTER XXV.

PREPARATIONS FOR INQUEST—JURORS AND WITNESSES.

ARTICLE 212.

CORONERS' JURIES—NUMBER AND QUALIFICATIONS.

[1] A CORONER'S jury must consist of twelve persons at least, and the inquisition must be found by twelve jurors at least, but the jury may and usually does consist of more than twelve, in which case the inquisition may be found by a majority consisting of twelve or more.

Coroners' juries must be composed of good and lawful men, and are generally composed of householders; but no special qualification is required by statute or otherwise.

Every man is presumed to be good and lawful till the contrary is proved.

If the death to be inquired into occurred in any of the Queen's palaces, the jury must be composed of yeomen officers of the household.

[2] If the death to be inquired into occurred in a prison, under the Prisons Acts of 1865 and 1877, officers of the prison, and prisoners confined in the prison, and every person engaged in any sort of trade or dealing with the prison, are disqualified from being jurors on any such inquest.

ARTICLE 213.

SUMMONING JURORS.

A coroner's jury is summoned in the following manner.

---

[1] Jervis, 200-201. It is obviously convenient to have an odd number, so that the case of an equal division, each party consisting of more than twelve, may not arise. The statute *De Officio Coronatoris* speaks of 4, 5, or 6 *vills*, but this has long become obsolete.

[2] 28 & 29 Vict. c. 126, s. 48; 40 & 41 Vict. c. 21, s. 44.

[1] The coroner issues a jury warrant to the peace-officer of the place where the body on which the inquest is to be held lies dead. The peace-officer issues summonses to a sufficient number of persons in his own, and if necessary the neighbouring, districts, to serve as jurors at the place and time appointed for the inquest.

ARTICLE 214.

ATTENDANCE OF JURORS.

[2] If any person having been duly summoned as a juror upon any coroner's inquest, as well of liberties and franchises contributing to the county rates as of counties, cities, and boroughs, does not, after being openly called three times, appear and serve as such juror, the coroner may impose upon him such fine as he thinks fit, not exceeding forty shillings.

[3] If any man having been duly summoned and returned to serve as a juror in any county in England or Wales, or in London, upon an inquest before a coroner, does not, after having been openly called three times, appear and serve as such juror, such coroner is authorized and required (unless some reasonable excuse is proved on oath or affidavit) to impose such fine upon him as he thinks fit, not exceeding five pounds.

[4] If any person having been duly summoned as a witness to give evidence upon any coroner's inquest does not, after being openly called three times, appear and give such evidence on such inquest, the coroner may impose upon him such fine as he thinks fit, not exceeding forty shillings.

---

[1] This is the modern practice. At common law the coroner might issue his warrant to the sheriff, and fine him if he did not return a panel. Jervis, 199.

[2] 7 & 8 Vict. c. 92, s. 17. The short result of these statutes is that a defaulting juror may in all cases be fined forty shillings, and in most cases five pounds, and a defaulting witness forty shillings in all cases.

[3] 6 Geo. 4, c. 50, s. 53.

[4] 7 & 8 Vict. c. 92, s. 17.

ARTICLE 215.

FINES HOW LEVIED.

[1] Upon any such fine as aforesaid being imposed, the coroner must make out and sign a certificate containing the name and surname, the residence and trade or calling of the person so making default, together with the amount of the fine imposed and the cause of such fine, and must transmit such certificate to the clerk of the peace for the district in which such defaulter resides, on or before the first day of the quarter sessions then next ensuing (and must, if the fine is imposed under the Act of Victoria, cause a copy of such certificate to be served upon the person so fined, by leaving it at his residence twenty-four hours at the least before the first day of the said quarter sessions). The clerk of the peace must copy the fine so certified on the roll on which all fines and forfeitures imposed at such quarter sessions are copied, and the same must be estreated, levied, and applied in like manner, and subject to the like powers, provisions, and penalties in all respects, as if such fine had been part of the fines imposed at such quarter sessions.

ARTICLE 216.

SUMMONING OF MEDICAL WITNESSES.

[2] If upon the holding of an inquest it appears to the coroner that the deceased person was attended at his death, or during his last illness, by any legally qualified medical practitioner, he may issue his order for the attendance of such practitioner as a witness at such inquest; and if it appears to the coroner that the deceased person was not attended at or immediately before his death by any such practitioner, he may issue such order for the attendance of any legally qualified medical practitioner being at the time

---

[1] 7 & 8 Vict. c. 92, s. 17, and 6 Geo. 4, c. 50, s. 53. The Act of Victoria is expressly stated to be cumulative as to any other powers which the coroner may ossess. Probably the Act of Geo. 4 is so also.

[2] 6 & 7 Will. 4, c. 89, ss. 1, 2.

in actual practice in or near the place where the death has happened. And the coroner, either in his order for the attendance of the medical witness, or at any time between the issuing of such order and the termination of the inquest may direct the performance of a post-mortem examination, with or without an analysis of the contents of the stomach or intestines, by the medical witness or witnesses who are summoned to attend at the inquest: provided that if any person states on oath before the coroner that in his belief the death of the deceased individual was caused partly or entirely by the improper or negligent treatment of any medical practitioner or other person, such medical practitioner or other person must not be allowed to perform or assist at the post-mortem examination of the deceased.

If it appears to the greater number of the jurymen sitting at any coroner's inquest that the cause of death has not been satisfactorily explained by the evidence of the medical practitioner or other witnesses who may be examined in the first instance, such greater number of jurymen may name to the coroner in writing any other legally qualified medical practitioner or practitioners, and require the coroner to issue his order for his or their attendance as witnesses, and for the performance of a post-mortem examination with or without an analysis of the contents of the stomach or intestines whether such an examination has been performed before or not. If the coroner refuses to issue such order he is guilty of a misdemeanor.

ARTICLE 217.

IF MEDICAL PRACTITIONER DOES NOT ATTEND.

[1] If any medical practitioner does not obey such order as aforesaid

when it has been personally served upon him; or

when he has received it in sufficient time to have obeyed it; or

when it has been served at his residence;

he must forfeit the sum of five pounds upon complaint

---

[1] 6 & 7 Will. 4, c. 89, s. 6.

thereof made by the coroner or any two of the jury before any two justices having jurisdiction in the parish or place where the inquest under which the order issued was held, or where the practitioner resides. The justices must enforce the penalty like other forfeitures, unless the practitioner shows a good and sufficient cause for his non-attendance.

ARTICLE 218.

DISINTERMENT OF BODY.

[1] The coroner may make an order for the disinterment of a body in order to holding an inquest thereon within a reasonable time after the death of the said body.

[1] 2 Hawk. P. C. 80; Jervis, 36.

CHAPTER XXVI.

PROCEEDINGS AT INQUEST.

Article 219.

COURT OF THE CORONER.

[1] THE Court held by the coroner at the taking of an inquest is an inferior Court of record.

[2] The coroner may commit for contempts committed in the presence of the Court.

[3] The coroner may exclude all persons from his Court if he thinks it desirable for the purposes of justice or decency.

[4] The coroner may adjourn the Court from time to time or place to place.

[5] The coroner usually permits counsel or solicitors to address the jury, or examine or cross-examine witnesses on behalf of persons likely to be accused of murder or manslaughter, or on behalf of any relation of the deceased person.

Article 220.

HOW IF INSUFFICIENT ATTENDANCE OF JURORS.

[6] If a sufficient number of jurors do not appear, the

---

[1] 4 Inst. 271.

[2] Jervis, 240a.

[3] Jervis, 228–31a.

[4] Jervis, 34.

[5] This may often be productive of hardship; e.g., a surviving relation, having malice against some one suspected of murder, and examined as a witness, may cross-examine that person so as to suggest his or her guilt, and bring to light matters of the most secret nature respecting his or her character without incurring the responsibility of making any direct accusation or instituting any active prosecution.

[6] Jervis, 204.

coroner may summon a sufficient number of good and lawful men from among those present or in the neighbourhood.

ARTICLE 221.

VIEW OF THE BODY.

[1] Every inquest must be held upon a view of the body on which the inquest is to be held, by the jury by which it is to be held; but they need not continue in the presence of the body for a longer time than is necessary to view it.

ARTICLE 222.

SWEARING THE JURY.·

The jury must be sworn either before they view the body or during the view.

ARTICLE 223.

CORONER TO TAKE DEPOSITIONS IN CASES OF MURDER OR MANSLAUGHTER.

[2] A coroner upon any inquisition before him taken whereby any person is indicted for manslaughter or murder, or as an accessory to murder before the fact, must put in writing the evidence given to the jury before him, or as much thereof as is material.

[3] In all cases it is the duty of the coroner to examine the witnesses who know anything as to the means by which the deceased came by his death.

ARTICLE 224.

CORONER'S POWER AT INQUEST TO SUMMON WITNESSES.

The coroner at the inquest may summon any person to give evidence, and if necessary may issue a warrant directing a peace-officer to bring any one before him as a witness, and if such person resists such warrant or refuses without suffi-

---

[1] Jervis, 200.
[2] 7 Geo. 4, c. 64, s. 4.
[3] Jervis, 206.

cient reason to give evidence, the coroner may commit him to prison for contempt.

ARTICLE 225.

DUTY TO HEAR ALL WITNESSES.

[1] The coroner is bound to hear all material ˉwitnesses, whether favourable or otherwise to any person suspected of an indictable offence.

ARTICLE 226.

SUMMING UP.

The coroner after hearing the evidence, and such observations by counsel or solicitors as he thinks fit to hear, ought to sum up the evidence to the jury.

ARTICLE 227.

VERDICT—HOW IF JURY DO NOT AGREE.

If the jurors, or a majority consisting of twelve jurors at least, agree in a verdict, the coroner must record it as hereinafter mentioned; [2] but if the jurors, or such a majority of them as aforesaid, are not able to agree, the coroner may adjourn them to the next assizes, when the judge will give his opinion and direction [? after re-hearing the evidence].

ARTICLE 228.

THE INQUISITION.

The coroner must, when the verdict is returned, record it in the form of an [3] inquisition, which must be signed by him, and by all the jurors, [4] by their marks if they cannot write, and it is usually sealed by the coroner and the jurors.

---

[1] 2 Hale, P. C. 60; Jervis, 221.

[2] This is a most unusual occurrence, and the practice on the matter seems unsettled. For instance, are the jury to be adjourned to the Central Criminal Court? Are the witnesses to be re-heard? Are they to be bound over to attend? Does this apply to cases in which no criminal charge is likely to be brought against any person?

[3] As to the requisites of an inquisition, see *post* in the chapter on Indictments.

[4] 6 & 7 Vict. c. 83, s. 2.

L

CHAPTER XXVII.

PROCEEDINGS SUBSEQUENT TO INQUEST.

ARTICLE 229.

WARRANT IN CASES OF MURDER AND MANSLAUGHTER.

[1] When the coroner's jury return a verdict of murder or manslaughter, it is the duty of the coroner to issue his warrant for the apprehension of the party accused, and to commit him to prison, or if he be already in prison, to issue a detainer to the gaoler in whose custody he is.

ARTICLE 230.

BAIL IN CASES OF MANSLAUGHTER.

[2] Where a coroner's jury has found a verdict of manslaughter against any person, the coroner before whom the inquest was taken may accept bail, if he thinks fit, with good and sufficient sureties for the appearance of the person so charged with manslaughter at the next assize and general gaol delivery to be holden in and for the county within which the inquest was taken and thereupon such person, if in custody of any bailiff or other officer of the coroner's Court, or in any gaol under a warrant of commitment issued by such coroner, must be discharged therefrom.

The coroner when he admits any person to bail must cause recognizances to be taken, and give a notice thereof to every person so bound, and must return such recognizances to the then next ensuing assizes.

---

[1] Jervis, 164.
[2] 22 Vict. c. 33, ss. 1, 2.

ARTICLE 231.

RECOGNIZANCES OF WITNESSES.

[1] When a verdict is returned by which any person is accused of murder or manslaughter or of being accessory to murder before the fact, the coroner has authority to bind all witnesses examined before him by recognizances, to appear at the next Court of oyer and terminer or gaol delivery at which the trial is to be, then and there to prosecute or give evidence against the party charged. Every such coroner must certify and subscribe the same evidence, and all such recognizances, and also the inquisition before him taken, and must deliver the same to the proper officer of the Court in which the trial is to be, before or at the opening of the Court.

[2] If the Director of Public Prosecutions gives notice to any coroner that he has instituted, or undertaken, or is carrying on any criminal proceeding, such coroner must transmit such depositions, recognizances, and inquisitions to the said Director, to be by him dealt with according to law.

ARTICLE 232.

DEPOSITIONS WHEN ADMISSIBLE AS EVIDENCE.

The admissibility of depositions taken by coroners on the trial of accused persons depends not on any statutory provision, but [3] on the common law rules relating to proof of evidence given on a former occasion.

ARTICLE 233.

COPIES OF DEPOSITIONS.

[4] At any time after all the depositions of the witnesses

---

[1] 7 Geo. 4, c. 64, s. 4.

[2] 42 & 43 Vict. c. 22, s. 5.

[3] Stephen's Digest Law of Evidence, Article 32.

[4] 22 Vict. c. 33, s. 3. This Act applies only to cases of manslaughter, the preamble stating that inconvenience has been caused by the coroner's inability to admit to bail in cases of manslaughter. The result is, that a prisoner committed by a coroner on a charge of manslaughter has a right to a copy of the depositions, but a prisoner so committed for murder has not.

have been taken, every person against whom any coroner's jury have found a verdict of manslaughter is entitled to have from the person having custody thereof copies of the depositions on which such verdict was found, on payment of a reasonable sum for the same, not exceeding the rate of three halfpence for every folio of ninety words.

ARTICLE 234.

CORONER TO BE PRESENT AT TRIAL.

[1] The coroner must be present in Court at the trial of any person charged with an offence by an inquisition taken before him, and if absent he may be fined.

---

[1] Jervis, 265 (4th cd.). *Re Urwin*, Old Bailey, 1827.

CHAPTER XXVIII.

OUTLAWRY.

ARTICLE 235.

WHEN A PERSON MAY BE OUTLAWED.

IF a person indicted cannot be otherwise compelled to appear, he may be outlawed; but as this process has practically become obsolete [1] the following general account of it is considered sufficient.

The first step in outlawry was, in the case of treason or felony, to issue a writ of *capias*; and though one *capias* was supposed to be sufficient, three such writs successively were usually issued on a return by the sheriff of *non est inventus*. The second writ was called *alias capias*, and the third *pluries capias*.

If the accused person could not be arrested, a writ was issued called an *exigent*, upon which the sheriff was to make five proclamations at five successive county Courts. If the accused person did not appear upon the fifth proclamation he was outlawed by the coroner.

In cases of misdemeanor the first step was a writ of *venire facias ad respondendum*. This was followed by a *distringas* or writ ordering the sheriff to compel the appearance of the party by seizing his land and taking its profits. An *alias* and *pluries distringas* might be issued. If this did not procure appearance, three writs of *capias*, and a writ of *exigent*, and five proclamations followed.

---

[1] In cases of great enormity extradition can now be almost always obtained. In minor cases compulsory banishment is a more severe punishment than a court of law would usually inflict. Few criminals possess property worth forfeiting.

[1] Judgment of outlawry upon an indictment for treason or felony is equivalent to and has all the effects of a conviction and attainder for treason or felony respectively, and involves [2] forfeiture.   The Act for the Abolition of Forfeitures for treason and felony does not apply to such forfeitures.

If the indictment is for misdemeanor, judgment of outlawry amounts only to a conviction for contempt in not answering the charge.

[1] Archb. 89 '
[2] 33 & 34 Vict. c. 23, s. 1.

PART VI.

CRIMINAL PLEADING.

CHAPTER XXIX.

[1]*INDICTMENTS DEFINED—THEIR DIVISION INTO COUNTS.*

ARTICLE 236.

INDICTMENT DEFINED.

An indictment is a written accusation of one or more persons of a crime preferred to and presented by a grand jury.

It may consist of one count or of more counts than one. If it consists of more counts than one, each count is considered as a separate indictment, and must fulfil all the requisites of an indictment hereinafter described.

ARTICLE 237.

JOINDER OF DIFFERENT PERSONS.

[2] In indictments for treason all persons who are principal traitors may be joined, whether they became such traitors before or after the overt acts charged in the indictment.

---

[1] For history of Indictments, see 1 Hist. Cr. Law, 273–294.
[2] Archb. 73; 2 Hale, 173.

In indictments for felony all principals in the first or second degree, and all accessories before or after the fact may be joined.

In indictments for misdemeanor all the principals may be joined, whether they became principals before or at the time of the actual commission of the offence.

[1] Any number of accessories at different times to any felony and any number of receivers at different times of property stolen at one time may be charged with substantive felonies in the same indictment, and may be tried together, notwithstanding the principal felon is not included in the same indictment or is not amenable to justice.

[2] Whenever any property is stolen, taken, extorted, obtained, embezzled, or otherwise disposed of in such a manner as to amount to a felony, either at common law or by virtue of the Larceny Act, 1861, any number of receivers at different times of such property or of any part thereof may be charged with substantive felonies in the same indictment and tried together, notwithstanding that the principal felon is not included in the same indictment, or is not in custody or amenable to justice.

An offence may be of such a nature that one person only can commit it, and in such cases every person who commits any such offence must be indicted separately.

Illustrations.

a. A instigates B to levy war against the Queen. B levies war accordingly, and is afterwards concealed from justice by C. A, B, and C may be indicted jointly.

b. A is accessory before the fact to a murder committed by B, and C is accessory after the fact to the same murder. They may be indicted jointly.

c. A and B each commit perjury by swearing to the same affidavit, in pursuance of a conspiracy to defraud. They must be separately indicted for perjury, but may be jointly indicted for the conspiracy to defraud.

---

[1] 24 & 25 Vict. c. 94, s. 6.
[2] 24 & 25 Vict. c. 96, s. 93.

ARTICLE 238.

EACH COUNT MUST CHARGE ONE OFFENCE AND NO MORE.

[1] Every count of an indictment must charge one offence and no more. But a count may charge more felonious acts than one, or felonious acts with respect to more persons than one, if such acts were all part of the transaction constituting the offence charged.

A count charging more offences than one is said to be bad for duplicity.

In indictments for burglary, the breaking and entering with intent to commit a felony, and the commission of the felony, may be charged in the same count.

[2] In an indictment for any embezzlement or for fraudulent application or disposition mentioned in sections 67, 68, 69 and 70 of the Larceny Act, 1861,[3] it is lawful to charge the offender with any number of distinct acts of embezzlement or fraudulent application or disposition, not exceeding three, which have been committed by him against her Majesty or against the same master or employer within the space of six months from the first to the last of such acts.

Illustrations.

1. A murders and robs B. He cannot be charged in the same indictment with murder and robbery.
2. A and B jointly assault C and D, and rob A of one shilling and B of two shillings, at the same time. A and B may be charged in the same indictment with assaulting C and D and robbing A of one shilling and B of two shillings.

ARTICLE 239.

WHEN MORE COUNTS THAN ONE.

Where there are more counts than one in an indictment they may either describe the same offence in different ways, or more offences than one either in one or in different ways.

---

[1] Archb. 68.

[2] 24 & 25 Vict. c. 96, s. 71.

[3] Archb. 69 ; *R.* v. *Purchase,* C. & Mar. 617 ; and cf. ss. 5 and 6 of the Larceny Act. The several acts are usually put in different counts.

ARTICLE 240.

SEVERAL COUNTS, ONE OFFENCE.

Any number of counts describing the same offence in different ways may be joined in the same indictment, provided that every offence so charged is either a felony of the same kind or a misdemeanor.

ARTICLE 241.

SEVERAL COUNTS, MORE FELONIES THAN ONE.

[1] Counts relating to different felonies ought not to be joined in the same indictment, except in the cases hereinafter mentioned. If they are so joined, the consequence stated in the next Article follows.

The cases above referred to are these :—

[2] Several counts may be inserted in the same indictment against the same person for any number of distinct acts of stealing, not exceeding three, committed by him against the same person within the space of six months from the first to the last of such acts.

[3] In any indictment containing a charge of feloniously stealing any property, a count or counts may be added for feloniously receiving the same or any part thereof, knowing the same to have been stolen, and in any indictment for feloniously receiving any property, knowing it to have been stolen, a count may be added for feloniously stealing the same.

ARTICLE 242.

IF DIFFERENT FELONIES JOINED, PROSECUTOR PUT TO ELECTION.

If it appears upon the trial of any indictment containing several counts for felony, that the counts relate to distinct offences and are not different ways of describing the same offence, the Court will [? may in its discretion] require the

---

[1] Archbold, 74–77.
[2] 24 & 25 Vict. c. 96, s. 5.
[3] Ibid. s. 92.

prosecutor to elect upon which charge he will proceed [? and may quash the other counts].

Provided that [1] if upon the trial of any indictment for larceny it appears that the property alleged in such indictment to have been stolen at one time was taken at different times, the prosecutor is not by reason thereof required to elect upon which taking he will proceed unless it appears that there were more than three takings, or that more than the space of six months elapsed between the first and the last of such takings, and in either of such last-mentioned cases the prosecutor must be required to elect to proceed for such number of takings, not exceeding three, as appear to have taken place within the period of six months from the first to the last of such takings.

ARTICLE 243.

SEVERAL COUNTS FOR MISDEMEANORS.

[2] Any number of counts either for the same or for different misdemeanors may be included in the same indictment.

[1] 24 & 25 Vict. c. 96, s. 6.
[2] Archbold, 77.

CHAPTER XXX.

OF THE CONTENTS OF AN INDICTMENT.

ARTICLE 244.

GENERAL RULE.

[1] AN indictment must state explicitly and directly, and not by way of recital, every fact necessary to constitute the offence charged, whether such fact is an external event or an intention or other state of mind, or a circumstance of aggravation affecting the legal character of the offence alleged, unless any such fact is necessarily implied by what is so expressly stated, and the contrary of everything not so expressed or implied will be presumed in favour of the person accused.

If an offence is founded upon the words of a statute, the indictment must follow the words of the statute, and if the clause of the statute creating the offence contains exceptions, the indictment must contain negative averments, showing that the case does not fall within such exceptions, whether the burden of proving that the case is so. excepted falls upon the defendant or not.

In indictments for crimes which have a known legal name the indictment must allege the commission of the crime, calling it by that name or using an adverb implying it.

The whole of the indictment must be written upon parch-

---

[1] This is the meaning of the rule, but in an indictment certainty to a certain extent in general is required. It might be expressed by saying that an indictment is the minor of a syllogism, of which the law on which it is founded is the major, and the guilt of the prisoner the conclusion. Scotch indictments are drawn in the syllogistic form. For these rules and the authorities on which they are founded see Archbold, 57 (as to certainties), 64–5 (as to statutory offences), 70 (as to repugnances).

ment in words and not in figures, except in the case of such documents as are set out in facsimile.

All the statements in an indictment must be consistent with each other.

These rules are subject to the exceptions specified in Art. 245, and to the powers of amendment specified in Art. 252.

Illustrations.

1. An indictment for high treason by compassing and imagining the Queen's death must state that the defendant traitorously compassed and imagined the Queen's death, and that in order to fulfil such compassing and imagination he did a certain overt act or acts, which must be stated in the indictment.

2. It was formerly necessary in an indictment for murder to describe the means by which the death was caused, as well as to say that the defendant murdered the deceased feloniously, wilfully, and of his malice aforethought.

3. An indictment for perjury must state (*a*) that there was a judicial proceeding before a competent authority; (*b*) that upon such proceeding it was a material question whether a certain thing was true; (*c*) that the defendant swore that it was or was not true corruptly and knowing the contrary; (*d*) that, in fact, what the defendant swore was false.

4. An indictment for obtaining goods under false pretences must state that the defendant obtained the goods by a certain pretence, which pretence must be set out, also that the pretence was false in fact.

5. [1] A statute punished the act of "unlawfully and maliciously setting fire to a barn." An indictment charged "feloniously, voluntarily, and maliciously" setting fire to a barn. This was insufficient.

6. The words "murder," "ravish," "steal, take, and carry," (or in the case of animals) "drive away," are necessary in indictments for murder, rape, and theft respectively. "Traitorously" and "burglariously" are necessary in indictments for high treason and burglary respectively.

7. [2] It is repugnant to say that a man was bound by a bond alleged to be forged, or to describe a person named for the first time as "the said A."

ARTICLE 245.

STATUTORY EXCEPTIONS TO THE PRECEDING ARTICLE.

(1.) [3] In any indictment for murder or manslaughter, or for being an accessory to any murder or manslaughter, it is not

---

[1] *R.* v. *Turner*, 1 Moo. C. C. 239; A. 65.

[2] 2 Hawkins, 315.

[3] 24 & 25 Vict. c. 100, s. 6.

necessary to set forth the manner in which, or the means by which the death of the deceased was caused, but it is sufficient in any indictment for murder to charge that the defendant did feloniously, wilfully, and of his malice aforethought, kill and murder the deceased ; and it is sufficient in any indictment for manslaughter to charge that the defendant did feloniously kill and slay the deceased ; and it is sufficient in any indictment against any accessory to any murder or manslaughter to charge the principal with murder or manslaughter (as the case may be) in the manner hereinbefore specified, and then to charge the defendant as an accessory.

(2.) [1] In every indictment for perjury, or for unlawfully, wilfully, falsely, fraudulently, deceitfully, maliciously, or corruptly taking, making, signing, or subscribing any oath, affirmation, declaration, affidavit, deposition, bill, answer, notice, certificate, or other writing, it is sufficient to set forth the substance of the offence charged, and by what Court, and before whom the oath, &c., was taken, made, signed, or subscribed, without setting forth the bill, answer, information, indictment, declaration, or any part of any proceeding, either in law or in equity, and without setting forth the commission or authority of the Court or person before whom such offence was committed ; [2] and in every indictment for subornation of perjury, or for corrupt bargaining or contracting with any person to commit wilful and corrupt perjury, or for inciting, causing, or procuring any person to commit any of the aforesaid offences, it is sufficient, wherever such perjury or other offence has been actually committed, to allege the offence of the person who actually committed such offence as aforesaid, and then to allege that the defendant unlawfully, wilfully, and corruptly did cause and procure the said person the said offence in manner and form aforesaid to do and commit; and wherever such perjury or other offence aforesaid has not been actually committed, it is sufficient to set forth the substance of the offence charged upon the defendant, without setting forth or averring any of the matters or things un-

[1] 14 & 15 Vict. c. 100, s. 20.
[2] Ibid s. 21.

necessary to be set forth or averred in the case of wilful and corrupt perjury as hereinbefore mentioned.

(3.) In indictments

(*a.*) [1] for obtaining or attempting to obtain by false pretences any property mentioned in the Larceny Act, 1861, s. 88, or

(*b.*) [2] for forging, altering, uttering, offering, disposing of, or putting off any instrument whatsoever, where it is necessary to allege an intent to defraud, or

(*c.*) [3] for any offence under the Falsification of Accounts Act, 1875,

it is sufficient to allege in general that the party did the act with intent to defraud, without alleging an intent to defraud any particular person.

(4.) [4] In indictments under 37 Geo. 3, c. 123, or 52 Geo. 3. c. 104 (the Unlawful Oaths Acts), for administering or causing to be administered or taken, or taking any oath or engagement therein mentioned, or being present at and consenting to the administering or taking thereof, it is not necessary to set forth the words of such oath or engagement, but it is sufficient to set forth the purport of such oath or engagement or some material part thereof.

(5.) [5] In indictments against any offender for being found at large contrary to the provisions of 5 Geo. 4, c. 84, or for rescuing or attempting to rescue or assisting in rescuing any such offender, it is sufficient to allege the order made for the transportation or banishment of such offender without charging or alleging any indictment, trial, conviction, judgment or sentence, or any pardon, or intention of mercy, or signification thereof, of or against, or in any manner relating to such offender.

(6.) [6] In an indictment for an offence under the Debtors Act, 1869, it is sufficient to set forth the substance of the offence charged in the words of the said Act, specifying the

---

[1] 24 & 25 Vict. c. 96, s. 88.

[2] 24 & 25 Vict. c. 98, s. 44.

[3] 38 & 39 Vict. c. 24, s. 2.

[4] 37 Geo. 3, c. 123, s. 4 ; 52 Geo. 3, c. 104, s. 5.

[5] 5 Geo. 4, c. 84, s. 23.

[6] 32 & 33 Vict. c. 62, s. 19.

offence, or as near thereto as circumstances admit, without alleging or setting forth any debt, act of bankruptcy, trading, adjudication, or any proceedings in, or order, warrant, or document of any Court acting under the Bankruptcy Act, 1869.

ARTICLE 246.

COMMENCEMENT OF INDICTMENTS.

The proper commencement of an indictment is

——⎱ the Jurors for our Lady the Queen upon their oath
to wit ⎰ present that

The ——⎱ is called the venue in the margin, and the
to wit ⎰ blank must be filled up by the name of the district over which the Court by which the indictment is to be tried has jurisdiction either under Chapter IX. or under Chapter X. The name may be that of any county or county of a city or town corporate, or of an assize county constituted under 39 & 40 Vict. c. 57, or 42 Vict. c. 1, or of the Central Criminal Court, or of any part or riding of a county, or of any borough to which the jurisdiction of the Court is limited.

ARTICLE 247.

NAMES OF THE DEFENDANT AND OF THE PERSON INJURED.

The indictment must state the Christian name or names and the surname of the defendant and the person against whom the offence was committed. If they have gone by or acknowledged more names than one, they may be described as J. S., otherwise called C. T.

If the name of both or either is unknown, he may be described as a person to the jurors unknown, but in this case he must be identified by some description, as for instance, a person personally brought before the jurors by the keeper of the prison, or a female infant child born of the body of A, and of the age of two days, and not named.

[1] The rank in life, occupation, and residence of the defen-

---

[1] By 1 Hen. 5, c. 5 (the Statute of Additions), it was necessary to state these matters, but by 14 & 15 Vict. c. 100, s. 24, it is enacted that no indictment shall be held insufficient " for want of or imperfection in the addition of any defendant.

dant need not be stated, but if the person injured has a name of dignity, he should be described by it.

[1] If a defendant when called upon to plead, pleads that he is wrongly named in any. indictment, the Court may, if satisfied by affidavit or otherwise of the truth of the plea, forthwith cause the indictment to be amended according to the truth, and the indictment does not abate, but the trial must proceed as if no such plea had been pleaded.

[2] If upon the trial of any indictment for any felony or misdemeanor there appears to be any variance in the Christian name or surname, or both Christian name and surname, of any person or persons whomsoever therein named or described, and if the Court considers such variance not material to the merits of the case, and that the defendant cannot be prejudiced thereby in his defence on such merits, it may order the indictment to be amended according to the proof.

ARTICLE 248.

DESCRIPTIONS OF THINGS IN INDICTMENTS—WRITTEN INSTRUMENTS.

[3] When written instruments form part of the gist of an offence charged, they must be set out *verbatim.*

[4] When an instrument is set out as having a certain purport, the meaning is that upon the face of it its legal effect is that which it is said to purport to be.

[5] When an instrument is set out in an indictment with the words "according to the tenor following," or "in the words and figures following," or the like, the meaning is that it is correctly recited though not so as to exclude misspelling.

When an instrument is set out in an indictment "in substance as follows," "to the effect following," or "in manner and form following," or the like, the meaning is that the writing is in substance what it is alleged to be.

[1] 7 Geo. 4, c. 64, s. 19.
[2] 14 & 15 Vict. c. 100, s. 1.
[3] Archb. 59.
[4] Archb. 60.
[5] Archb. 223.

M

Provided (1.) [1] that in any indictment for stealing, embezzling, destroying, or concealing, or for obtaining by false pretences any instrument, it is sufficient to describe such instrument by any name or designation by which the same may be usually known, or by the purport thereof, without setting out any copy or facsimile of the whole or any part thereof.

(2.) [2] That in all cases wherever it is necessary to make any averment in any indictment as to any instrument, whether the same consists wholly or in part of writing, print, or figures, it is sufficient to describe such instrument by any name or designation by which the same is usually known, or by the purport thereof, without setting forth any copy or facsimile of the whole or any part thereof.

(3.) [3] That in any indictment for forging, uttering, disposing, or putting off any instrument, or for engraving or making the whole or any part of any instrument, matter, or thing whatsoever, or for using or having the unlawful custody or possession of any plate or other material upon which the whole or any part of any instrument, matter, or thing whatsoever has been engraved or made, or for having the unlawful custody or possession of any paper upon which the whole or any part of any instrument, matter, or thing whatsoever has been made or printed, it is sufficient to describe such instrument, matter, or thing by any name or designation by which the same is usually known, without setting out any copy or facsimile of the whole or any part of such instrument, matter, or thing.

ARTICLE 249.

DESCRIPTION—WORDS.

[4] When words are the gist of an offence they must be specified in the indictment.

---

[1] 14 & 15 Vict. c. 100, s. 5.
[2] Ibid. s. 7.
[3] 24 & 25 Vict. c. 98, ss. 42, 43.
[4] Archb. 61.

ARTICLE 250.

DESCRIPTION—CHATTELS—MONEY.

[1] When personal chattels are the subject of an offence they must be described specifically by the names usually appropriated to them, and in cases of theft, or cases in which the value of the chattel is essential to the offence, a value must be assigned to them.

[2] In every indictment in which it is necessary to make any averment as to any money or any note of the Bank of England or any other bank, it is sufficient to describe such money or bank-note simply as money, without specifying any particular coin or bank-note, and such allegation, so far as regards the description of the property, may be sustained by proof of any amount of coin, or of any bank-note, although the particular species of coin of which such amount was composed, or the particular nature of the bank-note, is not proved; and in cases of embezzlement, or obtaining money or bank-notes by false pretences, by proof that the offender embezzled or obtained any piece of coin or any bank-note, or any portion of the value thereof, although such piece of coin or bank-note was delivered to him in order that some part of the value thereof should be returned to the party delivering the same or to any other person, and such part has been returned accordingly.

ARTICLE 251.

OWNERSHIP OF PROPERTY.

In indictments for offences committed upon any property the name of the owner of such property must be stated.

In the cases mentioned in the first column of the schedule hereto the property may, upon the authorities referred to in the third column, be laid in the persons mentioned in the second column.

[1] Archb. 43.
[2] 14 & 15 Vict. c. 100, s. 18.

M 2

SCHEDULE.

Bailee, offences with respect to property in the possession of.	The bailor or bailee. The person in whom the property is laid must have had either an actual or constructive possession.	Archb. 44; 2 Hale, 181; and see *R.* v. *Remnant*, R. & R. 136; *R.* v. *Adams*, R. & R. 225.
Banks, the property of joint-stock, carried on under the provisions of 7 Geo. 4, c. 46.	Any one of the public officers of such bank.	7 Geo. 4, c. 46, s. 9.
Bankrupt, offences with respect to the property of.	The trustee in bankruptcy, who may be called without naming him " the trustee of the property of A B, a bankrupt."	32 & 33 Vict. c. 71, 83, sub-s. 7.
Chelsea Hospital, offences with respect to the property of.	The Lords and others Commissioners of the Royal Hospital for Soldiers, at Chelsea, in the county of Middlesex.	7 Geo. 4, c. 16, s. 31.
Company registered under the Companies Act, 1862.	The corporate name of the company.	25 & 26 Vict. c. 89, s. 18.
Convicted felon undergoing his sentence.	The Queen.	*R.* v. *Whitehead*, 9 C. & P. 429, 2 Moo. C. C. 188.
Corporation.	The Corporation. A corporation created within memory must be described by the name by which it was incorporated, but an ancient corporation may by use have a special name by which it may be described.	*R.* v. *Patrick*, 3 East, P. C. 1059; 1 Leach, 253. Archb. 49, 10, Co. 87; 1 Leach, 523.
Corpse, stealing things buried with.	Executors or administrators, or, if there is neither, the person who paid the funeral expenses, or, if necessary, a person unknown.	2 Hale, 181; 2 East, P. C. 652.
County property, offences committed in respect of.	The inhabitants of such county (without specifying their names).	7 Geo. 4, c. 64, s. 15.
Customs officers, goods received by, as such.	The Queen.	39 & 40 Geo. 4, c. 36, s. 29.
Deceased persons, the property of intestate, before administration.	The judge of the Probate Division of the High Court.	21 & 22 Vict. c. 95, s. 19.

Friendly society or branch, the goods of.	The trustees for the time being, in their proper names as trustees for the society or branch (as the case may be), without further description, or the goods may, if stolen from the possession of any one who had the charge of them, be treated as goods stolen from bankers (v. *supra*).	38 & 39 Vict. c. 60, s. 16, sub-s. 5.
Highways, felony or misdemeanor in respect of tools, &c., used in repairing by the trustees or commissioners of a turnpike road, or by any other persons respectively.	Such trustees or commissioners, or the surveyors of highways.	7 Geo. 4, c. 64, s. 17. 7 Geo. 4, c. 64, s. 16.
Married woman, goods belonging to, except in the cases next following.	Her husband.	Common Law.
Where the husband and wife have been judicially separated.		20 & 21 Vict. c. 85, s. 25.
Where the wife has obtained a protection order under 20 & 21 Vict. c. 85.	The married woman.	20 & 21 Vict. c. 85, s. 21.
Where the property is the separate property of the wife under the Married Women's Property Act, 1882.		45 & 46 Vict. c. 75, s. 12.
Poor-house or workhouse, offences committed on or on the goods provided for the use thereof.	The overseers of the poor for the parish, without specifying their names.	7 Geo. 4, c. 64, s. 16.
Post-letters and telegraphic messages, offences with respect to.	The Postmaster-General.	7 Will. 4 & 1 Vict. c. 36, s. 40; 31 & 32 Vict. c. 110, s. 21; 32 & 33 Vict. c. 73, s. 23.[1]

[1] 31 & 32 Vict. c. 110 provides that a telegraphic message shall be the property of the Postmaster-General, and 32 & 33 Vict. c. 73 that it shall be deemed to be a post-letter within the meaning of 7 Will. 4 & 1 Vict. c. 36.

Public property stolen or embezzled by person in the public service.	The Queen.	24 & 25 Vict. c. 96, ss. 69, 70.
Several persons, offences concerning the joint property of.	One of the joint owners by name, adding, "and another or others," as the case may be.	7 Geo. 4, c. 64, s. 14.
Sewers, or matters subject to authority of commissioners of sewers, offences with respect to.	The commissioners of sewers, without naming them.	7 Geo. 4, c. 64, s. 18.
Telegraphic messages.	See "Post-letters."	
Trade-union registered, offences with respect to the property of.	The person or persons for the time being holding the office of trustee in their proper names as trustees of such trade-union, without any further description.	34 & 35 Vict. c. 31, s. 8.
Unknown person, offence with respect to or to the goods of.	A person to the jurors unknown.	2 Hale, 181.

ARTICLE 252.

POWER TO AMEND MISSTATEMENTS.

[1] Whenever, on the trial of any indictment for any felony or misdemeanor, there appears to be any variance between the statement in such indictment and the evidence offered in proof thereof,

In the name of any county, riding, division, city, borough, town corporate, parish, township, or place mentioned, or described therein; or

In the name and description of any person or persons, or body politic or corporate, therein stated or alleged to be the owner or owners of any property, real or personal, which forms the subject of any offence charged therein; or

In the name and description of any person or persons, body politic or corporate, therein stated or alleged to be injured or damaged, or intended to be injured or damaged, by the commission of such offence; or

---

[1] 14 & 15 Vict. c. 100, s. 1. The section seems not to apply to indictments for treason.

In the christian name or surname, or both christian name and surname, or other description whatsoever, of any person or persons whomsoever therein named or described ; or

In the name and description of any matter or thing whatsoever therein named or described; or

In the ownership of any property named or described therein,

The Court, before which the trial is had, may, if it considers such variance not material to the merits of the case, and that the defendant cannot be prejudiced thereby in his defence on such merits, order such indictment to be amended according to the proof by some officer of the Court or other person, both in that part of the indictment wherein such variance occurs, and in every other part of the indictment which it becomes necessary to amend, on such terms, as to postponing the trial to be had before the same or another jury, as the Court thinks reasonable.

After any such amendment the trial must proceed whenever the same is proceeded with in the same manner in all respects, and with the same consequences, both with respect to the liability of the witnesses to be indicted for perjury and otherwise, as if no such variance had occurred.

ARTICLE 253.

TIME.

[1] Every indictment states the day and year on which, and the place at which, the offence is supposed to have been committed; but a variance between the statement and the proof in respect of time is immaterial, unless the time is of the essence of the offence, or unless it is necessary that the indictment shall be preferred within a certain time after the offence.

[2] No indictment is insufficient for omitting to state the time at which any offence was committed in any case where time is not of the essence of the offence, nor for stating the

---

[1] Archb. 50–51.

[2] 14 & 15 Vict. c. 100, s. 24.

time imperfectly, nor for stating the offence to have been committed on a day subsequent to the finding of the indictment, or on an impossible day, or on a day that never happened.

Illustrations.

1. A is indicted for burglary committed between 9 on the night of 1 Jan. and 6 A.M. on Jan. 2, 1881. It is necessary to prove that the offence was committed between the hours of 9 and 6, but unnecessary to prove that it was committed on the day stated.

2. A is indicted for treason by adhering to the Queen's enemies on a given day. It need not be proved that he did so on the day mentioned, but it must be proved that he did so within three years of the indictment being found.

ARTICLE 254.

PLACE.

[1] Every indictment must state the place at which the offence is said to have been committed, but a variance between the statement and the proof is immaterial if it appears in evidence that the offence was committed in some place over which the Court had jurisdiction either generally, or by reason of the nature of the offence itself.

ARTICLE 255.

CONCLUSION.

An indictment for an offence against a statute usually ends " against the form of the statute, [or statutes,] in that case made and provided, and against the peace of our Lady the Queen, her Crown and her dignity."

An indictment for an offence at common law usually ends " against the peace of our Lady the Queen, her Crown and her dignity."

[2] No indictment can be held insufficient for want of a proper or formal conclusion.

---

[1] Archb. 51.
[2] 14 & 15 Vict. c. 100, s. 23.

CHAPTER XXXI.

MOTIONS TO QUASH INDICTMENTS—DEMURRERS—PLEAS—
MOTIONS IN ARREST OF JUDGMENT.

ARTICLE 256.

COURSES OPEN TO DEFENDANT PUT TO ANSWER TO AN INDICTMENT.

A DEFENDANT, when put to answer to an indictment, may either

Move to quash the indictment, or

Demur to the indictment, or

Plead to the indictment;

and, when a verdict has been given against him, he may move in arrest of judgment.

ARTICLE 257.

MOTION TO QUASH AN INDICTMENT.

Either a defendant or a prosecutor may move the Court, before which an indictment is to be tried, or the Queen's Bench Division of the High Court, to quash an indictment.

If the indictment is so defective, on the face of it, that no judgment could be given upon it even if the defendant were convicted; or

If counts have been joined in it, which, by law, ought not to have been joined, in which case the Court may, in its discretion, quash one or more of such counts.

[1] In these cases the motion may be made at any time before verdict.

If the application is made by the prosecutor, the Court will

---

[1] *R. v. Jones,* 12 C. & M. 87.

quash the indictment if the prosecution appears to be proper, and to be carried on in good faith; but in such cases a new bill must have been preferred and found against the defendant for the same offence, and such terms, as to costs and disclosure of the prosecutor's name, as the Court thinks just may be imposed upon the prosecutor.

All motions to quash indictments are motions addressed to the discretion of the Court, which may, if it thinks proper, leave the defendant to demur, or move in arrest of judgment.

Illustrations.

Indictments have been quashed—

1. When it appeared that the Court before which they were to be tried had no jurisdiction over the offence imputed ;

2. Where the language of a count was too general ;

3. Where a material allegation (as the existence of an intent to defraud) was omitted ;

4. Where in an indictment for libel the expressions imputed were not *primâ facie* libellous, and were not shown to be so by innuendoes or averments ;

5. Where two counts were joined charging distinct acts of obtaining goods by false pretences, one of which was not authorized by the Vexatious Indictments Act, the Court for Crown Cases Reserved held the second count ought to be quashed.

ARTICLE 258.

[1] DEMURRER.

The defendant may demur to an indictment—

(*a.*) On the ground that admitting the facts alleged against him to be true, they do not constitute any legal offence ; or

---

[1] It results from this and the following Article that demurrers are practically useless. 'A demurrer for a formal defect can at most lead to an amendment. A demurrer for a substantial defect is less advantageous than a motion in arrest of judgment, because in the latter case the defendant has the chance of an acquittal. Demurrers, therefore, are useful only in the case of substantial defects which would be cured by a verdict, and such cases are very rare, and even then the demurrer, if successful, would lead in almost any conceivable case to no result except a new indictment.

As for formal defects, it is difficult to say how, in the present state of the law, such a defect could occur. The defects which used to give rise to demurrers were all declared to be immaterial by 14 & 15 Vict. c. 100, s. 24. They consisted in the omission or misuse of formal averments 'not having the fear of (*b.*) On the ground of any formal defect, patent on the face of the indictment.

[1] Every objection to any indictment for any formal defect, apparent on the face thereof, must be taken either by demurrer or motion to quash such indictment before the jury is sworn, and not afterwards ; and every Court before which any such objection is taken for any formal defect, may, if it be thought necessary, cause the indictment to be forthwith amended in such particular by the officer of the Court, or other person, and thereupon the trial shall proceed as if no such defect had appeared.

The judgment on a demurrer to an indictment for felony, whether in favour of the Crown or of the defendant, is final.

The judgment on a demurrer to an indictment for misdemeanor is also final if it is for the defendant. If it is for the Crown it is final, unless the Court allows the defendant to plead over.

ARTICLE 259.

WHAT DEFECTS ARE CURED BY VERDICT.

[2] In indictments for offences at common law, where an averment is on the face of it imperfect, but is of such a nature that the verdict could not have been returned unless evidence of the matter not averred had been given, the defect in the averment is said to be cured by the verdict, and cannot be taken advantage of in arrest of judgment.

[3] Where the offence charged has been created by any statute, or subjected to a greater degree of punishment, or excluded from the benefit of clergy by any statute, the indictment must, after verdict, be held sufficient to warrant the punishment prescribed by the statute, if it describe the offence in the words of the statute.

God before his eyes,' 'at the special instigation of the devil,' 'as appears by the record,' 'with force and arms,' 'against the peace,' 'against the form of the statute' or 'statutes,' and various other matters. No article is founded on this enactment because it merely sweeps away a number of unmeaning technicalities.

[1] 14 & 15 Vict. c. 100, s. 25.

[2] Arch. 67–8.

[3] 7 Geo. 4, c. 64, s. 21.

Illustration.

[1] A was indicted for obtaining goods by false pretences. The indictment showed the words of the statute, but did not set out the false pretence. Held sufficient, after verdict, as the indictment, though demurrable, was good on a motion in arrest of judgment.

ARTICLE 260.

PLEAS.

The defendant may plead either to the jurisdiction or in abatement, or in bar.

ARTICLE 261.

PLEAS TO THE JURISDICTION.

A plea to the jurisdiction is proper only when the plea shows that the defendant is subject to the jurisdiction of some Court, other than that in which the plea is pleaded, but is improper if he denies that he is subject to any jurisdiction at all.

Illustrations.

1. A is indicted for murder at the Quarter Sessions. [2] A plea to the jurisdiction would be proper.

2. [3] A was indicted (before the Territorial Waters Jurisdiction Act) at the Central Criminal Court for an offence committed on a foreign ship on the high seas, within three miles of the coast. His defence was that the Court had no jurisdiction, but the proper plea was not a plea to the jurisdiction, but not guilty.

ARTICLE 262.

PLEAS IN ABATEMENT.

If a peer of parliament, indicted for felony, is arraigned elsewhere than before the House of Lords or in the Court of the Lord High Steward, he may plead his peerage in abatement.

[1] *R.* v. *Goldsmith,* L. R. 2 C. C. R. 74.

[2] In practice the indictment would not be found, or if it were it would be quashed on motion.

[3] *R.* v. *Keyn,* L. R. 2 Ex. Div. 63.

[1] If an indictment is found by a Grand Jury of which any member is disqualified, the fact may be pleaded in abatement.

The judgment for the Queen in a plea of abatement in misdemeanors is final, in treason and felony that the defendant answer over.

The judgment for the defendant, in a plea of abatement, is that the indictment be quashed.

ARTICLE 263.

PLEAS IN BAR.

There are four pleas in bar, namely, not guilty, autrefoits acquit, autrefoits convict, and pardon.

ARTICLE 264.

THE PLEA OF NOT GUILTY.

The plea of not guilty is pleaded by the defendant personally on his arraignment, by word of mouth, in the words " not guilty."

In the case of criminal informations and prosecutions for misdemeanor, removed into the Queen's Bench Division by *certiorari*, whether ordered to be tried at nisi prius or not, the plea may be pleaded in writing at the Crown office.

By pleading not guilty, the defendant puts in issue every material averment in the indictment, and under the plea he may prove any matter relevant to his guilt, whether by way of traverse, or by way of confession and avoidance.

ARTICLE 265.

PLEAS OF AUTREFOITS ACQUIT AND AUTREFOITS CONVICT.

The defendant may plead that he has been lawfully convicted or acquitted, as the case may be, of the offence charged in the indictment.

The plea should be on parchment, signed by counsel in a

---

[1] *R.* v. *Sheridan,* 31 St. Tr. 543–574.

proper form, but such a plea is, in point of form, sufficient[1] if the defendant says when called upon to plead that he has been lawfully convicted or acquitted of the offence charged in the indictment.

[2] In order to prove a plea of autrefoits convict, the defendant must show that he was previously convicted, either of the offence charged in the indictment to which the plea is pleaded, or of an offence of which he might be convicted on that indictment, and such proof is not made out by proof that the defendant was convicted on an indictment set aside on writ of error.

In order to prove a plea of autrefoits acquit, the defendant must prove that he was previously acquitted, either of the offence charged in the indictment to which the plea is pleaded, or that he was previously acquitted of some offence of which he might be convicted on that indictment, and such proof is not made out by proof of an acquittal upon a record containing any defect such that the defendant was not, by law, liable to suffer judgment for the offence charged against him in the first indictment.

A plea of autrefoits convict or acquit is sustained by proof of a previous conviction or acquittal in a foreign country.

In cases of misdemeanor judgment for the Crown on pleas of autrefoits convict or acquit is final.

In cases of felony or treason the defendant is permitted to plead not guilty as well, and, after judgment for the Crown, the case proceeds on the plea of not guilty.

Judgment for the defendant in all cases is final.

In the case of indictment for assault, a plea that the matter had been previously disposed of in a summary way under 24 & 25 Vict. c. 100, ss. 44, 45, would [probably] be good.

Illustrations.

1. A pleads autrefoits convict or acquit to an indictment for the murder of B, and proves a previous conviction or acquittal for the manslaughter of B, or for the concealment of the birth of B. The plea is proved.

---

[1] 14 & 15 Vict. c. 100, s. 28.
[2] See cases collected in Archbold 141-2.

2. A pleads autrefoits convict or acquit to an indictment for the murder of B, and proves a previous conviction or acquittal for wounding B with intent to murder. The plea is not proved.

3. [1] A pleads autrefoits acquit to an indictment for forging a will, set out in the indictment as beginning with the words " John Styles," &c. This plea is not proved by proving an acquittal upon an indictment in which the will was set out as beginning " I John Styles," &c.

ARTICLE 266.

PLEA OF PARDON.

The defendant may plead that he has been pardoned by her Majesty for the offence charged against him. Such pardon must be either under the Great Seal,[2] or if for felony, under the Queen's Sign Manual, countersigned by a Secretary of State, in which case, if the pardon is free, the prisoner must be discharged from custody, or if it is conditional, the condition must be performed before the pardon has the effect of a pardon under the Great Seal.

ARTICLE 267.

PLEA IN CASES OF LIBEL.

[3] On the trial of any indictment or information for a defamatory libel, the defendant having pleaded such plea as hereinafter mentioned, the truth of the matters charged may be inquired into, but does not amount to a defence unless it was for the public benefit that the said matters charged should be published. To entitle the defendant to give evidence of the truth of such matters charged, as a defence to such indictment or information, it is necessary for the defendant, in pleading to the said indictment or information, to allege the truth of the said matters charged in the manner required at the passing of Lord Campbell's Libel Act (24th August, 1843), in pleading a justification to an action

---

[1] *R.* v. *Coogan*, 1 Leach, 448; A. 143. In this case the prisoner was acquitted for the variance. Under the present law the variance would probably have been amended, and the first acquittal would have been a bar to any subsequent indictment.

[2] 7 & 8 Geo. 4, c. 28, s. 13.

[3] 6 & 7 Vict. c. 96, s. 6. See 2 Hist. Cr. Law, 384.

of defamation, and further to allege that it was for the public
benefit that the said matters charged should be published,
and the particular fact or facts by reason whereof it was for
the public benefit that the said matters charged should be
published, to which plea the prosecutor is at liberty to reply
generally denying the whole thereof.   The truth of the
matters charged in the alleged libel complained of by such
indictment or information, may, in no case, be inquired into
without such plea of justification.

In addition to such plea it is competent to the defendant
to plead a plea of not guilty.

The defendant is entitled to any defence under the plea of
not guilty, which it was competent to the defendant to make
under such plea to any action, or indictment, or information
for defamatory words or libel, on the 24th of August, 1843.

ARTICLE 268.

PLEA OF GUILTY.

A plea of guilty operates as a confession of the truth of all
the matters charged in the indictment.   It is usually
pleaded in person by the defendant saying the word "guilty"
on his arraignment, but in prosecutions in the Queen's Bench
Division it may be pleaded in writing at the Crown Office.

ARTICLE 269.

MOTION ON ARREST OF JUDGMENT.

If the indictment is so defective in substance that no
judgment can be given upon it [1] even after verdict, the defendant may, even after pleading guilty, move that judgment
may be arrested.   If the motion succeeds, the defendant is
discharged.

[1] See above Article 259.

CHAPTER XXXII.

OF THE PROOF OF INDICTMENTS, AND OF VERDICTS UPON THEM.

ARTICLE 270.

HOW MUCH OF AN INDICTMENT MUST BE PROVED.

IT is necessary to prove so much of an indictment as is sufficient to show that an offence charged in it has been committed within the local jurisdiction of the Court before which the trial takes place, or in some place over which that Court has jurisdiction with respect to that offence.

Averments, which are not necessary to the proof of these matters, are, even if material, surplusage, and need not be proved, but if an unnecessary averment is descriptive of the identity of anything which it is necessary to describe in the indictment, it must be proved as laid, but if it is not it may be amended.

Illustrations.

1. A is indicted for high treason, and several overt acts of treason are alleged. It is sufficient if any one of them is proved.
2. A is indicted for having forged and caused to be forged. It is sufficient if either is proved.
3. A is indicted for libelling with two separate intentions. Proof of either is sufficient.
4. A is indicted for stealing numerous articles specified. Proof of his stealing any one is sufficient.
5. A is indicted for stealing a black horse. The averment that the horse was black must be proved, but if it appears that the horse was not black the indictment may be amended by omitting the word "black."

ARTICLE 271.

EFFECT OF VARIANCES.

If there is a variance between any of the averments necessary to support a conviction and the evidence given in

N

support of it, the prisoner is entitled to be acquitted, unless the variance is one which may be, and is, amended by the Court.

Illustration.

A is indicted for the murder of John Taylor. The evidence is that he murdered James Taylor. A is entitled to be acquitted, [1] unless the Court sees fit to amend the indictment.

ARTICLE 272.

ANY OFFENCE CHARGED IN THE INDICTMENT MAY BE PROVED.

If the whole of the offence charged in the indictment is not proved, but so much of it as to constitute an offence is proved, the defendant may be acquitted of the offence charged, and convicted of the offence proved, [2] provided that each offence is either felony or misdemeanor; but a defendant indicted for felony or misdemeanor cannot be convicted on that indictment for misdemeanor or felony respectively, nor can a person, indicted for an offence upon a given set of facts, be convicted upon that indictment of an offence of a different nature from that which the indictment charges, except in the cases expressly excepted in Articles 273–275.

Illustrations.

1. A is indicted for the murder of B. The killing of B is proved, but not the malice aforethought. A may be acquitted of murder, and convicted of manslaughter.

2. A is indicted for burglariously breaking and entering B's house with intent to steal between 9 P.M. and 6 A.M. The time at which A broke and entered is not proved, but the rest of the indictment is proved. A may be acquitted of burglary and convicted of house-breaking.

3. A is indicted for robbing B of five shillings. A may, according to the proof, be convicted of robbery, of stealing from the person, or of simple larceny.

4. A is indicted for feloniously ravishing B. He cannot be convicted of

---

[1] Such an amendment would be made as a matter of course if the variance was the result of a mere mistake as to the name, but if John Taylor and James Taylor were altogether different people, killed under different circumstances, the amendment would be refused.

[2] Archb. 231.

the misdemeanor of indecent or common assault, though the fact may prove it.

5. A is indicted for feloniously ravishing B. He cannot be convicted upon that indictment of the felony of abduction with intent to marry or carnally know B, though the facts may prove it.

ARTICLE 273.

WHEN PERSONS INDICTED FOR FELONY MAY BE CONVICTED OF MISDEMEANOR.

In the following cases persons indicted for felony may be convicted of misdemeanor.

(1.) [1] If on the trial of any person charged with any felony or misdemeanor it appears to the jury upon the evidence that the defendant did not commit the offence charged, but that he was guilty only of an attempt to commit the same, such person is not by reason thereof entitled to be acquitted, but the jury are at liberty to return as their verdict that the defendant is not guilty of the felony or misdemeanor charged, but is guilty of an attempt to commit the same.

(2.) [2] If any person tried for the murder of any child is acquitted thereof, it is lawful for the jury to find, in case it so appears in evidence, that the child had recently been born, and that such person did, by some secret disposition of the dead body of such child, endeavour to conceal the birth thereof.

(3.) [3] If upon the trial of any felony except murder or manslaughter, where the indictment alleges that the defendant did cut, stab, or wound any person, the jury are satisfied that the defendant is guilty of the cutting, stabbing, or wounding charged in such indictment, but are not satisfied that the defendant is guilty of the felony charged in such indictment, the jury may acquit the defendant of such felony, and find him guilty of unlawfully cutting, stabbing, or wounding.

[1] 14 & 15 Vict. c. 100, s. 9.
[2] 24 & 25 Vict. c. 100, s. 60.
[3] 14 & 15 Vict. c. 19, s. 5.

ARTICLE 274.

INDICTMENT FOR ONE FELONY CONVICTION FOR ANOTHER.

In the following cases persons indicted for one felony may be convicted of another.

(1.) [1] If upon the trial of any person upon any indictment for robbery it appears to the jury upon the evidence that the defendant did not commit the crime of robbery, but that he did commit an assault, with intent to rob, the defendant is not by reason thereof entitled to be acquitted, but the jury are at liberty to return as their verdict that the defendant is guilty of an assault, with intent to rob.

(2.) [2] If upon the trial of any person for embezzlement or fraudulent application, or disposition of property under the Larceny Act, 1861, it is proved that he took the property in question in any such manner as to amount in law to larceny, he is not by reason thereof entitled to be acquitted, but the jury are at liberty to return as their verdict that such person is not guilty of embezzlement or fraudulent application, or disposition, but is guilty of simple larceny, or of larceny as a clerk, servant, or person employed for the purpose or in the capacity of a clerk or servant, or as a person employed in the public service, or in the police, as the case may be; and if upon the trial of any person indicted for larceny it is proved that he took the property in question in any such manner as to amount in law to embezzlement or fraudulent application, or disposition as aforesaid, he is not by reason thereof entitled to be acquitted, but the jury are at liberty to return as their verdict that such person is not guilty of larceny, but is guilty of embezzlement, or fraudulent application, or disposition, as the case may be.

ARTICLE 275.

INDICTMENT FOR MISDEMEANOR—PROOF OF FELONY.

In the following cases a person may be convicted of misdemeanor upon proof of felony.

[1] 24 & 25 Vict. c. 96, s. 41.
[2] Ibid s. 72.

(1.) [1] If upon the trial of any person for any misdemeanor it appears that the facts given in evidence amount in law to a felony, such person is not by reason therof entitled to be acquitted of such misdemeanor, and no person tried for such misdemeanor is liable to be afterwards prosecuted for felony on the same facts, unless the Court, before which such trial is had, thinks fit, in its discretion, to discharge the jury from giving any verdict in such trial, and to direct such person to be indicted for felony, in which case such person may be dealt with in all respects as if he had not been put upon his trial for such misdemeanor.

(2.) [2] If upon the trial of any person indicted for the misdemeanor of obtaining any chattel, money, or valuable security by false pretences, it is proved that he obtained the property in question in any such manner as to amount in law to larceny, he is not by reason thereof entitled to be acquitted of such misdemeanor.

[1] 14 & 15 Vict. c. 100, s. 12.
[2] 24 & 25 Vict. c. 96, s. 88.

PART VII.

ARRAIGNMENT—TRIAL—APPEAL.

CHAPTER XXXIII.

ARRAIGNMENT—PLEA—CHALLENGES OF JURORS.

ARTICLE 276.

RIGHT TO BE TRIED.

[1] ANY person committed for treason or felony plainly and specially expressed in the warrant of commitment may make a prayer or petition in open court in the first week of the sittings, or on the first day of the sessions of oyer and terminer or gaol delivery to be brought to his trial. If he is not indicted at some time in the next sittings or sessions of oyer and terminer and gaol delivery after his commitment, the judges must upon motion made on the last day of such sittings or sessions admit him to bail, unless it appears

---

[1] 31 Ch. 2, c. 2, s. 6. The style is modernized. This is the Habeas Corpus Act of 1679. The section in question makes no provision for persons indicted of or committed for misdemeanor. They are entitled to be bailed under the earlier provisions of the Act. In a few words the result is this : A person charged with misdemeanor can be bailed till trial at Common Law, and under the Habeas Corpus Act (see Art. 136) a person committed for treason or felony can insist upon being indicted at the first sessions after his committal, and if he is not tried upon being bailed, unless the witnesses for the Crown cannot appear, he can at the second sittings insist on his release without bail unless he is tried.

upon oath that the witnesses for the Crown could not be produced at those sittings or sessions. If any person committed as aforesaid is not indicted and tried at the second sittings or sessions after his commitment, or is acquitted, he must be discharged.

ARTICLE 277.

ARRAIGNMENT—STANDING MUTE.

When an indictment, or inquisition, has been found against any person, and the time for his trial is come, he must be called to the Bar of the Court; the substance of the indictment, or inquisition, must be stated to him, and he must be asked whether he pleads guilty or not guilty.

In the case of criminal informations, filed in the Queen's Bench Division of the High Court, the defendant may, and generally does, plead by attorney by making an entry in a book kept for that purpose in the Crown office.

If, upon being arraigned, the defendant does not answer directly, or keeps silence, he is said to stand mute, and a jury must be impannelled to try whether he stands mute of malice, or by the visitation of God.

[1] If the jury find that he stands mute of malice, or if he refuses to plead, the Court may order a plea of not guilty to be entered on behalf of such person.

[2] If the jury find that he stands mute by the visitation of God, but that he can be made to understand the proceedings, and can plead by signs, the plea can be demanded and can be taken by signs.

[3] If the jury find that he cannot understand the proceedings, the prisoner must be confined, during her Majesty's pleasure, as if he were insane.

If, at any time during the proceedings, the jury find that the prisoner is not in such a state of mind as to be able to understand the proceedings and make his defence, the prisoner must be detained during her Majesty's pleasure.

---

[1] 7 & 8 Geo. 4, c. 28, s. 2.
[2] *R. v. Pritchard*, 7 C. & P. 303 ; approved in *R. v. Berry.*
[3] *R. v. Berry*, 1 Q. B. D. 447.

ARTICLE 278.

PLEA OF GUILTY.

If the defendant pleads guilty he is in the same position as if he was convicted by the verdict of the jury.

ARTICLE 279.

PLEA OF NOT GUILTY.

If the defendant pleads not guilty, the officer of the Court proceeds to call the jury, by whom the crime is to be tried, from the pannel returned by the sheriff for that purpose.

ARTICLE 280.

CHALLENGES TO THE ARRAY.

[1] The defendant may challenge the array, that is to say, he may allege that the pannel is unfairly returned, and ought to be quashed.

The ground of the challenge may be either that some fact exists inconsistent with the impartiality of the sheriff, or other officer returning the pannel, or that some fact exists which makes it improbable that he should be impartial, or that some fact exists which does, in fact, interfere with his impartiality.

The challenge must be in writing, and must set forth the fact on which it is grounded.

The Court must decide whether the alleged fact is in itself a good cause of challenge, in which case it is called a principal challenge, or whether it is merely a fact from which partiality may or may not be inferred, in which case it is called a challenge to the favour, or that the sheriff has been guilty of some default in returning the pannel.

If the Court holds that the alleged fact is a good cause for a principal challenge, and the alleged fact is denied, or if the Court holds that the alleged fact is good as a challenge to the favour, and either the fact or the partiality sought to be inferred from it, or both are denied, two triers must be appointed by the Court to try the facts in dispute. If the

[1] Archb. 163-7.

triers find in favour of the challenge, the pannel is quashed, and a new one is ordered to be returned by the coroners or other officers. If they find against the challenge, the pannel is affirmed.

ARTICLE 281.

PEREMPTORY CHALLENGES.

In cases of treason, the prisoner may challenge peremptorily thirty-five jurymen.

In cases of felony, the prisoner may challenge peremptorily twenty jurymen.

In cases of misdemeanor, the prisoner has no right to any peremptory challenge.

ARTICLE 282.

CHALLENGES FOR CAUSE.

[1] In all cases the Crown and the defendant may challenge any number of jurors for cause. Such challenges may be either principal challenges or challenges to the favour.

If such a challenge is made, the matter of fact in issue must be tried by two triers. If jurors have been sworn at the time when the challenge is made, the two jurors last sworn are sworn as triers. If no juror has been sworn, two persons appointed by the Court are sworn as triers. If one juror has been sworn, that juror acts with two triers appointed by the Court. If the triers find in favour of the challenge, the juror objected to is not sworn. If they find against the challenge, he is sworn.

ARTICLE 283.

WHEN CHALLENGES MUST BE MADE.

When the defendant intends to challenge peremptorily, he has a right to have the pannel of jurors called over before he makes any challenge, that he may know who answer.

The jurymen are then called, and as they come to the book to be sworn, and before they are sworn, the challenges must be made.

[1] Archb. 167-9

A challenge is too late if made after the words of the oath are repeated, but before the book is kissed.

[1] The prosecutor need not show the cause of any challenge for the Crown until the whole of the pannel has been gone through, and he may require any juror whom he challenges for the Crown to stand by, that is to say, to wait till all the jurors available at the time when the pannel is called over, have been called. If a full jury is not then sworn, the prosecutor must show the cause of his challenges for the Crown, and if he fails to do so the jurors challenged for the Crown must be sworn.

ARTICLE 284.

OTHER PLEAS THAN GUILTY OR NOT GUILTY.

When the defendant pleads any plea other than not guilty, and an issue of fact is joined thereon, the truth of the plea must be tried by a jury impannelled for that purpose.

[2] It seems, but it is not certain, that in such cases no peremptory challenges are allowed.

---

[1] *Mansel* v. *Reg.*, 8 E. & B. 64; and see 6 Geo. 4, c. 50, s. 29, as explained by this case.

[2] 2 Hale, P. C. 267; 2 Hawk. 570, book 2, c. 43, s. 6.

CHAPTER XXXIV.

[1] *TRIAL.*

ARTICLE 285.

PROCLAMATION AND GIVING IN CHARGE.

WHEN a jury has been sworn, and the defendant has pleaded not guilty, proclamation is made, calling upon the prosecutor and witnesses to prosecute and give their evidence, for the prisoner stands on his deliverance.

In cases of treason and felony the officer of the Court then gives the prisoner in charge to the jury, stating the effect of the indictment, or inquisition, and the prisoner's plea of not guilty, and charging them to determine whether he is guilty or not.

ARTICLE 286.

OPENING THE CASE.

The counsel for the prosecution then opens the case to the jury.

ARTICLE 287.

EVIDENCE FOR THE PROSECUTION.

Having opened the case, the counsel for the Crown examine the witnesses for the prosecution, who are afterwards cross-examined and re-examined according to the rules of evidence.

ARTICLE 288.

DEFENCE BY COUNSEL.

[2] In all cases whatever prisoners, charged with any crime,

---

[1] For a history of the growth of the system of trial, see 1 Hist. Cr. Law, ch. xi. p. 319–427. For a description of modern criminal trials, see ch. xii. p. 428–456.

[2] As to felonies, see 6 & 7 Will. 4, c. 114. As to treason, 7 & 8 Will. 3, c. 3. As to misdemeanors, the right existed at common law.

are admitted, after the close of the case for the prosecution, to make full answer and defence thereto by counsel learned in the law, or by solicitors in Courts where solicitors practise as counsel.

ARTICLE 289.

WITNESSES FOR PRISONER.

After the defence, [1] witnesses for the prisoner may be examined on oath, in all respects, in the same manner as witnesses for the Crown.

ARTICLE 290.

SUMMING UP OF COUNSEL.

[2] If any prisoner or defendant is defended by counsel but not otherwise, it is the duty of the presiding judge, at the close of the case for the prosecution, to ask the counsel for each prisoner or defendant so defended by counsel whether he intends to adduce evidence, and in the event of none of them thereupon announcing his intention to adduce evidence, the counsel for the prosecution must be allowed to address the jury a second time in support of his case, for the purpose of summing up the evidence against such prisoner or defendant; and upon every trial for felony or misdemeanor, whether the prisoner or defendant or any of them is defended by counsel or not, each and every such prisoner or defendant, or his counsel, must be allowed, if he thinks fit, to open the case, and after the conclusion of such opening, or of all such openings, if there be more than one, such prisoner or defendant, or their counsel, is entitled to examine such witnesses as he may think fit, and when the evidence is all concluded to sum up the evidence.

ARTICLE 291.

REPLY.

If witnesses are called, or evidence is given on behalf of

---

[1] 1 Anne, c. 9, s. 3.   [2] 28 Vict. c. 18, s. 2.

the prisoner, the counsel for the prosecution has the right to reply, [1] even if the evidence is evidence to character only.

The Attorney-General, or the Solicitor-General, appearing for the Crown in his official capacity, has the right of reply, whether the prisoner gives evidence or not.

[2] It has been doubted whether this right extends to counsel instructed to appear as the representative of the Attorney-General by any department of Government.

ARTICLE 292.

SUMMING UP BY JUDGE.

After the reply, the judge sums up the case to the jury.

ARTICLE 293.

JURY CONSIDER THEIR VERDICT.

After the summing up, the jury consider their verdict, and may, if they please, retire for that purpose from the Court.

If they do so, a bailiff is sworn to keep them in some private place without meat, or drink, or fire—candlelight excepted—and neither to speak to them himself (except to ask if they are agreed on their verdict), nor to suffer any other person to speak to them without the leave of the Court.

[3] The judge may allow the jury the use of a fire, and reasonable refreshment to be procured at their own expense.

ARTICLE 294.

VERDICT MUST BE UNANIMOUS—CASE OF NOT AGREEING.

The verdict of the jury must be unanimous.   [4] If the jury

---

[1] But in such cases the right is never, or hardly ever, exercised.

[2] I lately admitted the Solicitor-General's right to reply, but the authorities are not quite uniform.   Erle, J., permitted Mellor, J. (then at the Bar), to reply, when instructed for the Attorney-General by the Treasury, in *Reg.* v. *Garner*, at Lincoln Assizes in 1857.   In Hensay's case in 1758 the Solicitor-General replied, though no witnesses were entered for the prisoner, 19 St. Tr. 1378.

[3] 33 & 34 Vict. c. 77, s. 23.

[4] *Winsor* v. *Reg.*, L. R. 1 Q. B. 289.

are unable to agree, the Court may discharge them, in which case the prisoner must be recommitted and tried by another jury.

ARTICLE 295.

VERDICT OF NOT GUILTY.

If the jury return a verdict of not guilty, the Court may direct the prisoner to be discharged if there is no other indictment against him, but [1] he is not entitled, by law, to be discharged until the end of the sittings when his trial takes place.

ARTICLE 296.

VERDICT OF GUILTY.

If the jury return a verdict of guilty in a case of felony, the prisoner is asked whether he has anything to say why sentence should not be passed upon him.

In cases of misdemeanor for which the defendant is indicted in the Court before which he is tried, he may be sentenced immediately upon his conviction.

In either case the prisoner or defendant may move in arrest of judgment on the ground of any defect in the indictment which is not cured by the verdict. If such a motion is successful, the Court will set aside the proceedings and give judgment of acquittal. If no such motion is made, or if, being made, it fails, the Court in all cases, except the case of the trial of records in the High Court (Queen's Bench Division), proceeds to pass sentence either at once, or at such subsequent time during the sittings as it thinks proper.

ARTICLE 297.

CONVICTION ON RECORD FROM THE HIGH COURT (QUEEN'S BENCH DIVISION).

Upon a trial for felony or misdemeanor upon any record

---

[1] This is the practical effect of 31 Ch. 2, c. 2, s. 7 (the Habeas Corpus Act, 1679). The language is to the effect that if a person committed for trial is not indicted before the end of the sittings for which he is committed he must be discharged.

of the High Court (Queen's Bench Division), the judge before whom the verdict is taken may, upon a verdict of guilty :

(*a.*) Abstain from passing sentence, and leave the prosecutor to move the Court for judgment at its next sittings, taking bail from the person convicted to appear to receive judgment or committing him to prison, or

(*b.*) [1] Pronounce judgment during the sittings, or assizes, at which the trial is held, as well upon any person who has suffered judgment by default, or confession, upon the same record as upon those who have been tried and convicted, whether such persons are present or not in Court, excepting only where the prosecution is, by information, filed by leave of the Queen's Bench Division, or such cases of information by the Attorney-General, wherein the Attorney-General prays that judgment may be postponed. The judgment so pronounced must be indorsed upon the record of nisi prius, and afterwards entered upon the record in Court, and is of the same force and effect as a judgment of the Court, unless the Court, within six days after the commencement of the ensuing term, grants a rule to show cause why a new trial should not be had, or the judgment amended. And the judge before whom the trial is had, may either issue an immediate order or warrant for committing the defendant in execution, or respite the execution of the judgment upon such terms as he thinks fit, until the sixth day of the ensuing term ; in case imprisonment is part of the sentence, he may order the period of imprisonment to commence on the day on which the party shall be actually taken to, and confined in, prison.

ARTICLE 298.

NOT GUILTY ON GROUND OF INSANITY.

[2] In all cases where it is given in evidence upon the trial of any person charged with treason, murder, felony, or [3] misdemeanor, that the prisoner was insane at the time of

---

[1] 11 Geo. 4, and 1 Will. 4, c. 70, s. 9.

[2] 39 & 40 Geo. 3, c. 94, s. 1.

[3] Effect of 3 & 4 Vict. c. 54, s. 3.

the commission of such offence, and such person is acquitted, the jury must find specially whether such person was insane at the time of the commission of such offence, and declare whether such person was acquitted by them on the ground of such insanity. If they find that such person was insane at the time 'of committing such offence, the Court before whom such trial is had must order such person to be kept in strict custody, in such manner as to the Court seems fit, until her Majesty's pleasure shall be known.[1]

ARTICLE 299.
PREGNANCY OF FEMALE PRISONER.

When any woman has been sentenced to death she may say, in arrest of execution, that she is pregnant, whereupon the Court must direct a jury of twelve matrons to be empannelled to try whether or not [2] she be with child of a quick child. If it is found that she is, she must be respited until she is delivered, or until it is no longer possible in the course of nature that she should be delivered.

ARTICLE 300.
ADJOURNMENT.

From the time when the prisoner is given in charge to the jury in cases of felony, and from the commencement of the statement of the counsel for the Crown in cases of misdemeanor, the trial must proceed continuously, subject to a power on the part of the Court [3] to adjourn the hearing from day to day, or for a longer period, and subject also to the power of the Court mentioned in the next Article.

 In cases of treason and felony, the jury must be kept to-

---

[1] The section goes on to empower the Queen to give an order for the confinement of such person during her Majesty's pleasure.

[2] Form of oath in Archb. 193.

[3] Adjournments from day to day, or over Sunday, are of constant occurrence. In *Reg.* v. *Orton* the Court habitually adjourned from Friday to Monday, and in some instances for several days, once even for a fortnight or more, in order that a certain witness's evidence might be tested

gether, and must be prevented from communicating, without the leave of the Court, with any person from the time when the prisoner is given into their charge till the verdict is given. When it is necessary to adjourn, from day to day in such cases, the Court makes order for the proper accommodation of the jury at the expense of the public.

ARTICLE 301.

POWER TO DISCHARGE THE JURY.

[1] If the judge, or a juryman, dies or is taken ill during the trial, or if owing to any tumult, fire, or other accident, it is impossible, or would be improper, to proceed with the trial, the Court may discharge the jury and commit the prisoner to custody to be tried at some subsequent time.

[2] If a juror misconducts himself, as by separating from his fellows without leave, and if it appears to the Court that his conduct though improper was not corrupt and did not affect his impartiality, the juror is liable to be fined for contempt, but the verdict is good. If misconduct on the part of the jury is brought to the knowledge of the Court before their verdict is given, it seems that the Court may in its discretion discharge them, and have the case tried by another jury. [3] If misconduct on the part of the jury (as by taking bribes) is discovered after verdict and judgment, it seems that the jury may be punished, but the verdict and judgment cannot be reversed.

[1] In the case of the illness of a juryman it is not uncommon to swear a new juryman, giving the prisoner his challenges over again, and to read over the Judge's notes of the evidence given, swearing the witnesses afresh, and asking them if the evidence so recorded is true, the prisoner having power to cross-examine further. The circumstances may be such that this is unobjectionable, but where the first jury is discharged because it is unable to agree a second trial so conducted was disapproved of, though it was not set aside as a mistrial. See *Reg.* v. *Bertrand,* L. R. 1 P. C. 520. (The case occurred in New South Wales, but was brought on appeal before the Judicial Committee of the Privy Council.)

[2] 2 Hale P. C. 296, and see *R.* v. *O'Neil,* 3 Crawford & Dix. (Circuit Cases) 146.

[3] I can give no direct authority for this, but it seems to follow from the fact that it would not be error in the record, nor a question of law arising on the trial.

ARTICLE 302.

PRISONER'S RIGHT TO BE PRESENT.

The prisoner has a right to be present at the trial so long as he conducts himself properly, but the Court may, in its discretion, permit his absence in cases of misdemeanor, and may proceed with the trial in his absence in cases in which he has pleaded to an indictment or information in the High Court (Queen's Bench Division).

[1] If a prisoner so misconducts himself as to make it impossible to try him with decency, the Court, it seems, may order him to be removed and proceed in his absence.

---

[1] I have never known or heard of this being done, but Lord Cranworth (then Rolfe, B.) threatened to have Rush removed from Court, at his trial for murder at Norwich in 1849, if he persisted in a singularly indecent and outrageous course of cross-examination. I have heard from eye-witnesses an account of a trial before Shee, J. (then acting as Commissioner), at Dorchester, where the prisoner (a convict at Portland, tried for the murder of a warder) behaved with such desperate violence that it was necessary to fasten him down with chains and straps. He was not, however, removed from the Court, and it is obvious that in capital cases, or indeed, in any trial involving severe punishment, almost any measures, short of removing the prisoner, should be resorted to.

CHAPTER XXXV.

¹PROCEEDINGS BY WAY OF APPEAL.

ARTICLE 303.

WRIT OF ERROR.

² A WRIT of error is a writ issuing from the common law side of the Chancery Division of the High Court of Justice to the judge, or judges, of an inferior Court requiring him or them to send the record and proceedings of the indictment, inquisition, or information, on which judgment has been pronounced, and in which error is alleged, to the Court authorized to review the same.

The writ of error cannot issue without the fiat of the Attorney-General. In cases of misdemeanor the High Court (Queen's Bench Division) will direct him to give the fiat if it is made to appear to the Court that any question of law, which ought to be argued, has arisen upon the procedure followed.

In cases of treason and felony the Court will not interfere with the discretion of the Attorney-General as to issuing a writ of error.

ARTICLE 304.

DRAWING UP THE RECORD—ASSIGNMENT OF ERROR— JOINDER—CONCILIUM.

When a writ of error issues, the record of the case to which it relates must be drawn up by the officer of the Court in

---

¹ See 1 Hist. Cr. Law, 308–18.

² Archb. 202–15. I have given only such of the points in the procedure as are necessary, in order to understand its general purpose and effect. The practice on the subject is very minute and technical, both as to the steps to be taken to obtain the writ, and as to the matter to be set out in the record, and the manner of stating it.

which the indictment, information, or inquisition is. The record is a history of the whole of the proceedings in the case containing the indictment and the judgment of the Court, and stating every step taken in the proceedings, and in particular any order or act of the Court alleged to have been improper or irregular, but the evidence of the witnesses, the decision of the judge as to the admission or rejection of any point of it, and the direction of the judge to the jury can in no case appear upon the record.

When the record is drawn up it is certified by the inferior Court to the High Court (Queen's Bench Division), upon which the defendant must assign error by stating, in writing, the objections which he makes to the course taken, and appearing on the record. In cases of treason or felony the defendant must for this purpose appear personally in Court.

An order is then made for an argument which is called a concilium.

The errors assigned are then argued before the Court, and judgment is given.

ARTICLE 305.

JUDGMENT ON A WRIT OF ERROR.

The judgment upon a writ of error is either for the Crown, that the judgment of the Court below be affirmed; or for the defendant, that the judgment of the Court below be [1] set aside.

[2] It is competent for a Court of Error reversing any judgment on any criminal case either to pronounce the proper judgment or to remit the record to the Court below, in order that such judgment may be pronounced.

---

[1] "Reversed, annulled, and held as entirely void, and that the defendant be restored to all things which by the judgment aforesaid he has lost, and that he may go thereof without day." Form in Archb. 215.

[2] 11 & 12 Vict. c. 78, s. 5; and see *Holloway* v. *Reg.* 17 Q. B. 317. In *Reg.* v. *O'Connell* there was one judgment on many counts, some of which were bad, though others were good, and would have warranted the judgment. The judgment was set aside, and the enactment referred to was passed in order to enable judgment to be pronounced in such cases.

ARTICLE 306.

APPEAL IN WRITS OF ERROR.

An appeal lies from the judgment of the High Court (Queen's Bench Division) upon a writ of error [1] in regard to any error in law apparent upon the record, as to which no question has been reserved for the judges in the Court for Crown Cases Reserved, to the Court of Appeal, and from the decision of the Court of Appeal to the House of Lords.

ARTICLE 307.

BAIL IN ERROR IN CASES OF MISDEMEANOR.

[2] In every case of judgment for a misdemeanor where the defendant has obtained a writ of error to reverse such judgment, execution thereupon must be stayed until such writ of error is finally determined; and in case the defendant is imprisoned under such execution, or any fine has been levied either in whole or in part in pursuance of such judgment, the said defendant is entitled to be discharged from imprison· ment, and to receive back any money levied on account of such fine from the person in whose possession the same is, until such final determination as aforesaid. Execution cannot be stayed upon any such judgment unless and until the defendant be bound by [3] recognizance with two sufficient sureties to prosecute the writ of error with effect, [4] and personally to appear in the Court wherein such writ is returnable on the day whereon judgment shall be given upon the said writ of error, and also if so ordered by the Court, four days notice being given to the defendant, or his solicitor, and the

---

[1] 36 & 37 Vict. c. 66, s. 47.

[2] 8 & 9 Vict. c. 68, s. 1.

[3] The recognizances must be acknowledged by a judge of the Queen's Bench Division, or a commissioner appointed to take special bail in actions in the High Court. The sureties alone are enough if the defendant is under legal disability. The clerk of the Crown must deliver to the defendant a certificate of the recognizances, which is a warrant to the gaoler to discharge the defendant from prison, or to any person in possession of money paid as a fine to repay it to the defendant.

[4] 16 & 17 Vict. c. 32, s. 1.

bail, and so from day to day, and not to depart that Court without leave, and forthwith to render the said defendant to prison according to the said judgment in case the said judgment shall be affirmed.[1]

ARTICLE 308.

WHERE JUDGMENT IS AFFIRMED UPON WRIT OF ERROR— PERIOD OF IMPRISONMENT.

[2] Where a defendant appears personally as aforesaid, and the judgment is affirmed or the writ of error quashed, the Court may commit the defendant to the keeper of the Queen's prison, to be by him delivered to the keeper of the prison in which he was adjudged to be confined.

[3] The term of imprisonment (if any) in such a case is reckoned to begin from the day when the defendant is actually in custody in the prison in which he was adjudged to be imprisoned, and if the defendant was discharged from imprisonment on giving bail in error, he must be imprisoned for such further period in the same prison as, with the time during which he has already been imprisoned under the same execution, will be equal to the period for which he was adjudged to be imprisoned.

ARTICLE 309.

JUDGE'S WARRANT TO TAKE IN EXECUTION.

[4] Where it appears to a judge of the Queen's Bench Division by affidavit or certificate of the proper officer of the Court of error, that the recognizance of a defendant given as aforesaid has been ordered to be estreated, or that the judgment has been affirmed upon writ of error, or the writ of error quashed, and that default has been made for four days in rendering the defendant to prison, the judge may issue his

---

[1] No judgment may be reversed upon writ of error for want of joinder in error, or otherwise, except by order of the Court.   16 & 17 Vict. c. 32, s. 3.

[2] 16 & 17 Vict. c. 32, s. 4.

[3] Ibid. s. 6.

[4] Ibid, s. 5.

warrant under his hand and seal to apprehend the defendant, and convey him to the prison in which he was adjudged to bo imprisoned.[1]

ARTICLE 310.

RESERVING QUESTIONS OF LAW FOR THE JUDGES.

[2]Any question of law arising upon the trial of any person for any offence at any Court of Oyer and Terminer, or General Gaol Delivery, or Quarter Sessions, may be reserved by the Judge, Commissioner, justices of the peace, [[3] or recorder,] before whom the case is tried, if he or they think fit to do so, for the opinion of the judges of the Queen's Bench Division of the High Court of Justice, as hereinafter mentioned.

[3] Such questions may relate to the reception of evidence, the direction given by the judge to the jury, or to matter appearing on the record and forming the subject of a motion in arrest of judgment,[4] but not to matters raised on demurrer, or to irregularities of practice which may constitute a mistrial.

ARTICLE 311.

CASE HOW RESERVED.

[5] The judge, or Commissioner, or Court of Quarter Sessions reserving a question as mentioned above must state, in a case signed in the manner usual before the passing of 11 & 12 Vict. c. 78 (31st August, 1848), the question or questions of law which have been so reserved with the special circumstances upon which the same have arisen, and such case

---

[1] In such a case the defendant must pay the costs of the render to prison so enforced, upon the prosecutor having them ascertained by the Master of the Queen's Bench Division on the Crown side and delivering to the defendant and to the keeper of the prison the Master's certificate of the amount, and must be kept in prison till he does. The Court may estreat the recognizances by rule or order without issuing a *scire facias.* 16 & 17 Vict. c. 32, ss. 7, 8.

[2] 11 & 12 Vict. c. 78, s. 1.

[3] *R.* v. *Masters,* 1 Den. C. C. 332.

[4] *R.* v. *Faderman,* 1 Den. C. C. 565, *R.* v. *Mellor,* D. & B. C. C. 468,

[5] 11 & 12 Vict. c. 78, s. 2.

must be transmitted to the said judges of the Queen's Bench Division of the High Court.

ARTICLE 312.

TRIAL OF QUESTIONS SO RESERVED.

[1] The questions of law reserved as mentioned in Articles 261-2, must be determined by the judges of the Queen's Bench Division of the High Court, or five of them at the least, of whom the Lord Chief Justice of England must be one, [2] unless by writing under his hand, or by the certificate in writing of his medical attendant, it appears that he is prevented, by illness or otherwise, from being present at any Court duly appointed for the purpose aforesaid, in which case his presence at such Court is not necessary. No appeal lies from the judgment of the said High Court in any criminal case or matter, save for some error of law apparent upon the record as to which no question has been reserved for the consideration of the said judges under 11 & 12 Vict. c. 78.

ARTICLE 313.

JUDGMENT TO BE GIVEN IN OPEN COURT.

[3] The judgment or judgments of the said judges must be delivered in open Court after hearing counsel or the parties, in case the prosecutor or the person convicted thinks it fit that the case shall be argued.

ARTICLE 314.

POWERS OF THE JUDGES.

[4] The said judges of the Queen's Bench Division of the High Court may reverse, affirm, or amend any judgment which has been given on the indictment or inquisition on the trial whereof the question reserved arose,

[1] 36 & 37 Vict. c. 66, s. 47.
[2] 44 & 45 Vict. c. 68, s. 15.
[3] 11 & 12 Vict. c. 78, s. 3.
[4] Ibid. s. 2.

or may avoid such judgment and order an entry to be made on the record that in their judgment, the party convicted ought not to have been convicted,

or may arrest the judgment,

or may order judgment to be given thereon at some other session of oyer and terminer, or gaol delivery, or other sessions of the peace, if no judgment has been before that time given, as they are advised,

or may make such other order as justice may require,

[1] or may cause the case or [2] certificate to be sent back for amendment, and thereupon the same must be amended accordingly, and judgment must be delivered after it has been amended.

ARTICLE 315.

CERTIFICATE OF JUDGMENT OR ORDER.

[3] The judgment or order of the said judges must be certified under the hand of the Lord Chief Justice to the clerk of assize, or clerk of the peace, or the deputy of either of them as the case may be, who must enter the same on the original record in proper form.

ARTICLE 316.

PROCEEDINGS UPON CERTIFICATE.

[4] A certificate of such entry under the hand of the clerk of assize or clerk of the peace or deputy, as the case may be, must be delivered. or transmitted by him to the sheriff or gaoler. in whose custody the person convicted is. The said certificate is a sufficient warrant to such sheriff or gaoler and all other persons for the execution of the judgment, as the same is so certified to have been affirmed or amended, and execution must be thereupon executed upon such judgment, and for the discharge of the person convicted from further

---

[1] 11 & 12 Vict. c. 78, s. 4.

[2] See next Article.

[3] 11 & 12 Vict. c. 78, s. 2.

[4] Ibid. s. 2. The proper form of this certificate is given in the schedule to the Act.

imprisonment if the judgment is reversed, avoided, or arrested, and in that case such sheriff or gaoler must forthwith discharge him, and also the next court of oyer and terminer and gaol delivery, or sessions of the peace, must vacate the recognizance of bail, if any, and if the court of oyer and terminer and gaol delivery, or court of quarter sessions is directed to give judgment the said court must proceed to give judgment at the next sessions.

ARTICLE 317.

NEW TRIAL IN CASES IN QUEEN'S BENCH DIVISION.

Where any misdemeanor is tried in the High Court (Queen's Bench Division), or is sent by the Court to be tried as a nisi prius record, the defendant after conviction may move for a new trial on any ground on which a new trial might be moved for in a civil case, as mis-reception or rejection of evidence, misdirection, or that the verdict was against the evidence. [1] No new trial will be granted if the defendant has been acquitted, even in case of an indictment for a proceeding substantially civil.

[2] In one case of felony tried as a nisi prius record a new trial was granted, but that case has been disapproved.

[1] *Reg.* v. *Duncan,* 7 Q. B. D. 198. In this case the defendant was acquitted upon an indictment for obstructing a highway sent by the Court to be tried as a nisi prius record.

[2] *R.* v. *Scaife,* 17 Q. B. 238 but see *R.* v. *Bertrand,* L. R. 1 P. C. 520, and *Reg.* v. *Duncan, supra.*

PART VIII.

COSTS—REWARDS—RESTITUTION OF PROPERTY.

CHAPTER XXXVI. — Costs in Criminal Cases.

CHAPTER XXXVII.—Rewards, Compensation, and Restitution of Property.

CHAPTER XXXVI.

[1] *COSTS IN CRIMINAL CASES.*

ARTICLE 318.

COSTS IN CASES OF FELONY.

[2] THE Court before which any person is prosecuted or tried for any felony may at the request of the prosecutor or of any person who appears on recognizance or subpœna to prosecute or give evidence against any person accused of any felony, order payment unto the prosecutor of the costs and expenses which such prosecutor has incurred in preferring the indictment, and also payment to the prosecutor and witnesses for the prosecution of such sums of money as to the Court seem reasonable and sufficient to reimburse such prosecutor and witnesses for the expenses they have severally incurred in attending before the examining magistrates and the grand jury, and in otherwise carrying on such prosecution, and also to compensate them for their trouble and loss of time therein.

Where no bill of indictment has been preferred it is still lawful for the Court where any person has in the opinion of

---

[1] 1 Hist. Cr. Law, 498-9.
[2] 7 Geo. 4, c. 64, s. 22.

the Court *bonâ fide* attended the Court, in obedience to any such recognizance or subpœna, to order payment unto such person of such sum of money as to the Court seems reasonable and sufficient to reimburse such person for the expenses which he or she has *bonâ fide* incurred by reason of attending before the examining magistrates, and by reason of such recognizance or subpœna, and also to compensate such person for trouble and loss of time.

The amount of expenses of attending before the examining magistrates and the compensation for trouble and loss of time therein must be ascertained by the certificate of such magistrates granted before the trial or attendance in court if they think fit to grant the same. The amount of all the other expenses and compensation must be ascertained by the proper officer of the court.

ARTICLE 319.

COSTS IN CASES OF MISDEMEANOR.

[1] Where any prosecutor or other person appears before any Court on recognizance or subpœna to prosecute or give evidence against any person indicted for any of the misdemeanors hereinafter mentioned, such Court may order payment of the costs and expenses of the prosecutor and witnesses for the prosecution together with a compensation for their trouble and loss of time in the same manner as the Courts may order the same in cases of felony as aforesaid ; and although no bill of indictment be preferred, it is still lawful for the Court where any person has *bonâ fide* attended the Court in obedience to any such recognizance, to order payment of the expenses of such person together with compensation for his trouble and loss of time in the same manner as in cases of felony.

The said misdemeanors are :—

[1] Assault with intent to commit felony.

[1] Attempt to commit felony.

[1] Riot.

[1] 7 Geo. 4, c. 64, s. 23.

[1] Any misdemeanor for receiving stolen property, knowing the same to have been stolen.

[2] Assault upon a peace-officer in the execution of his duty, or upon any person acting in aid of such officer.

[2] Neglect or breach of duty of a peace-officer.

[2] Assault committed in pursuance of any conspiracy to raise the rate of wages.

[2] Obtaining property by false pretences.

[2] Wilful and indecent exposure of the person.

[2] Perjury.

[2] Subornation of perjury.

[3] Carnally knowing and abusing any girl above ten and under twelve.

[3] Unlawfully taking or causing to be taken any unmarried girl under sixteen out of the possession and against the will of her father or mother or of any other person having the lawful care or charge of her.

[2] Conspiring to charge any person with or indict any person of any felony.

[3] Conspiring to commit felony.

[4] Any indictable misdemeanor against the Larceny Act, 1861, the Malicious Injuries to Property Act, 1861, the Forgery Act, 1861, or the Offences against the Person Act, 1861.

[5] In prosecutions for any offence against the Coinage Offences Act, 1861, in England which are conducted under the direction of the solicitors of the Treasury, the Court before which the offence is prosecuted or tried must allow the expenses of the prosecution in all respects as in cases of felony: and in all prosecutions for any such offence in England which are not so conducted, the Court may, in case a conviction takes place, but not otherwise, allow the expenses of the prosecution in like manner.

[1] 7 Geo. 4, c. 64, s. 23.
[2] Ibid. s. 22.
[3] 14 & 15 Vict. c. 55, s. 2.
[4] 24 & 25 Vict. c. 96, s. 121; 24 & 25 Vict. c. 97, s. 77; 24 & 25 Vict. c. 98, s. 54; 24 & 25 Vict. c. 100, s. 77.
[5] 24 & 25 Vict. c. 97, s. 42.

ARTICLE 320.

COSTS IN PARTICULAR CASES.

In the several cases mentioned in the first column of the following schedule costs are payable in the manner described in the second column by virtue of the statutory enactments referred to in the third column.

SCHEDULE.

Admiralty, felony and misdemeanor committed within the jurisdiction of	As if such felony or misdemeanor had been committed in the county in which the same is heard and determined, or if the same is heard and determined at the Central Criminal Court as if the same had been committed in the county of Middlesex. All sums properly so paid out of any county or other local rate must be repaid out of moneys provided by Parliament.	44 & 45 Vict. c. 55, s. 9.
Assault, convictions of, on indictment.	The Court may sentence the person convicted to pay the prosecutor's costs and an allowance for his time and trouble, and to be imprisoned until he does so for any time not exceeding three months, in addition to any other sentence which may be passed.	24 & 25 Vict. c. 100, s. 74.
Bankrupt prosecuted under the Act for the Abolition of Imprisonment for Debt, 1869.	The Court may order costs to be paid as in cases of felony.	32 & 33 Vict. c. 62. s. 17.
Companies, prosecution of directors, officers, &c., of, by order of Court, under the Companies Act, 1862.	If the Court subject to whose superior supervision the company is being wound up orders the prosecution, it may also	25 & 26 Vict. c. 89. s. 167.

	order the costs to be paid out of the assets. If the winding-up is altogether voluntary, and the Court has sanctioned the prosecution, the costs are payable out of the assets of the company.	25 & 26 Vict. c. 89, s. 168.
Corrupt practices at Parliamentary elections, prosecutions under 17 & 18 Vict. c. 102.	The Court may order payment to the prosecutor of his reasonable costs if before the finding of the indictment or the granting of the information he entered into a recognizance in £200, with two sureties, to prosecute with effect and pay the defendant's costs in case of an acquittal, and not otherwise. If the indictment or information is by a private prosecutor and the defendant is acquitted, the defendant is entitled to recover taxed costs from the prosecutor.	17 & 18 Vict. c. 102, ss. 10 & 13. 17 & 18 Vict. c. 102, s. 12.
Corrupt practices (of bribery, undue influence, or personation) at a municipal election.	Costs, expenses, and compensation for trouble and loss of time are payable to the prosecutor and his witnesses, unless the Court orders otherwise.	35 & 36 Vict. c. 60, s. 9.
Guardians, &c., overseers of the poor, prosecutions by, under s. 73 of the Offences against the Person Act, 1861.	The guardians, &c., may pay the costs out of the common fund of the Union or the fund in their hands.	24 & 25 Vict. c. 100, s. 73.
Libel, indictment or information by a private prosecutor.	If judgment is given for the defendant he is entitled to recover costs from the prosecutor. If the issue upon a special plea of justification is found for the prosecutor he is	6 & 7 Vict. c. 96, s. 8.

	entitled to recover from the defendant the costs he has sustained by reason of such plea.	
Personation, prosecution for, by returning officer under 35 & 36 Vict. c. 33, s. 24.	Costs, expenses, and compensation for trouble and loss of time must be allowed to the prosecutor and his witnesses in the same manner as they may be allowed in cases of felony.	35 & 36 Vict. c. 33, s. 24.
Poor laws, offences against, specified in s. 59 of the Poor Law Amendment Act, 1844.	The guardians may pay the costs out of the funds in their hands or the common fund of the Union.	7 & 8 Vict. c. 101, s. 59; 28 & 29 Vict. c. 79, s. 9.

ARTICLE 321.

COSTS OF WITNESSES FOR THE DEFENCE.

[1] The Court before which any accused person is prosecuted or tried, or for trial before which he is committed or bailed to appear for any felony or misdemeanor, may, in its discretion, at the request of any person who appears before such Court on recognizance to give evidence on behalf of the person accused, order payment unto such witness so appearing [of] such sum of money as to the Court seems reasonable and sufficient to compensate such witness for the expenses, trouble, and loss of time he has incurred or sustained in appearing before the necessary magistrate, and at or before such Court.

The amount of such expenses of attending before such examining magistrate, and compensation for trouble and loss of time therein must be ascertained by the certificate of such magistrate granted before the attendance in Court. The amount of all other expenses and compensation must be ascertained by the proper officer of the Court who must [2] make out and deliver to the person entitled thereto an order for such expenses and compensation upon such and the same

---

[1] 30 & 31 Vict. c. 35, s. 5.

[2] He was entitled by this statute to a fee of sixpence for doing so, but the practical result of 32 & 33 Vict. c. 89, s. 9, is to disentitle him to any fee.

treasurers and officers as are liable to payment of an order for the expenses of the prosecutor, and witnesses against such accused person, and if the Court has no power to order the expenses of the prosecutor, then upon the treasurer or other officer in the capacity of a treasurer of the district where the offence of such accused person is alleged to have been committed. Such treasurer or other officer must pay the same orders upon sight therof, and must be allowed the same in his accounts. Provided that in no case may any such allowances or compensation exceed the amount permitted to be made to prosecutors and witnesses for the prosecution, and that such allowances and compensation must he allowed and paid as part of the expenses of the prosecution.

ARTICLE 322.

COSTS OF ACCUSED PERSON WHEN PAID BY THE PROSECUTOR.

[1] Wherever any bill of indictment is preferred to any grand jury under the [2] Vexatious Indictments Act, 1859, against any person who has not been committed to or detained in custody or bound by recognizance to answer such indictment and the person accused thereby is acquitted thereon, the Court before which such indictment is tried may in its discretion direct and order that the prosecutor or other person by or at whose instance such indictment was preferred shall pay unto the accused person the just and reasonable costs, charges, and expenses of such accused person and his witnesses (if any) caused or occasioned by or consequent upon the preferring of such bill of indictment to be taxed by the proper officer of the Court.

If such costs are not paid within one calendar month of such order, the High Court or a judge thereof, or the justices and judges of the Central Criminal Court if the bill of indictment was preferred in that Court, may issue against the person on whom such order is made, such writ or process as might on the 1st of October, 1867, be lawfully issued by the

[1] 30 & 31 Vict. c. 35, s. 2.
[2] 22 & 23 Vict. c. 17.

P

superior Courts at Westminster or the Central Criminal
Court for enforcing judgments thereof.

ARTICLE 323.

COSTS, HOW PAID. COUNTIES.

[1] Every order for payment to any prosecutor or other person
as aforesaid must be forthwith made out and delivered by the
proper officer of the Court unto such prosecutor or other person
upon being paid for the same the sum of one shilling for the
prosecutor and sixpence for each other person and no more,
and except in the cases hereinafter mentioned must be made
upon the treasurer of the county, riding, or division in which
the offence was committed or is supposed to have been committed, who is authorized and required upon sight of every
such order forthwith to pay the person named therein or to
any one duly authorized to receive the same on his behalf the
money in such order mentioned, and must be allowed the
same in his accounts.

ARTICLE 324.

COSTS, HOW PAID.   PLACES NOT CONTRIBUTING TO THE
COUNTY RATES.

[2] All sums directed to be paid in respect of felonies, and
such misdemeanors as aforesaid committed or supposed to
have been committed in [3] districts which do not contribute to
the payment of any county rate must be paid out of the rate
in the nature of a county rate, or out or any fund applicable
to similar purposes, where there is such a rate or fund by the
treasurer or other officer having the collection or disbursement
of such rate or fund, and where there is no such rate or fund
in such district must be paid out of the rate or fund for the
relief of the poor of the parish, township, district, or precinct
therein where the offence was committed or supposed to have

---

[1] 7 Geo. 4, c. 64, s. 24.
[2] Ibid. s. 25.
[3] Liberties, franchises, cities, towns, and places.

been committed, by the overseers or other officers having the collection or disbursement of such last-mentioned rate or fund. The order of the Court must in every such case be directed to such treasurer, overseers, or other officers respectively instead of the treasurer of the county, riding, or division, as the case may require.

ARTICLE 325.

COSTS, HOW PAID.   ADMIRALTY DIVISION.

[1] The judge of the Admiralty Division of the High Court may in every case of felony and in every case of misdemeanor, such as are mentioned above, committed upon the high seas, order the assistant to the counsel for the affairs of the Admiralty and Navy, to pay such costs, expenses, and compensation to prosecutors and witnesses in like manner as other Courts may order the treasurer of the county to pay the same, and such assistant is authorized and required upon sight of every such order forthwith to pay the same to the person mentioned therein, or to any one duly authorized to receive the same on his behalf, the money in such order mentioned, and must be allowed the same in his accounts.

ARTICLE 326.

COSTS OF WITNESSES BEFORE MAGISTRATES.

[2] Any magistrate may, at his discretion, at the request of any prosecutor or other person who has appeared before him either by summons or otherwise, on a charge of felony *bonâ fide* made upon reasonable and probable cause, or on a charge in any case of the several misdemeanors enumerated in 7 Geo. 4. c. 64, s. 23, and of 14 & 15 Vict. c. 55, s. 2, *bonâ fide* preferred, and who has been examined on such charge of felony or misdemeanor, grant a certificate of the expenses

---

[1] 7 Geo. 4, c. 64, s. 27. The payment of costs in the same manner may be ordered by the judges of assize and commissioners of oyer and terminer and gaol delivery who have jurisdiction to try offences committed on the high seas. 7 & 8 Vict. c. 2, s. 1. See Articles 75 and 76.

[2] 29 & 30 Vict. c. 52, s. 1.

and of the amount to be allowed for trouble and loss of time
to the witnesses so appearing and examined on such charge
of felony or misdemeanor in the same manner and to the
same or like extent as magistrates are authorized by law to
do in cases of felony and in cases of misdemeanor enumerated
in the said Acts, where a committal for trial takes place, or
the parties are bound over by recognizance or subpœna to
prosecute and give evidence.

ARTICLE 327.

COSTS OF WITNESSES BEFORE MAGISTRATES—HOW PAID.

[1] Every examining magistrate signing or granting such
certificate must forward the same to the clerk of the peace
for the [2] district within which such petty sessional division
or district is situate to be laid by him before the next
quarter sessions of the peace for such district, and such
Court is at liberty to allow the amount, or so much of the
amount, named in the certificate on the same being certified
by the proper officer of the Court of quarter sessions as
correct, and thereupon to sign an order for payment on the
treasurer or other officer of the district in which the offence
was committed, or supposed to have been committed, in the
same manner as an order for payment would have been made
in case the parties had been bound over to prosecute and an
indictment had been preferred, and such treasurer or other
person must pay the amount of such order to the person
named therein.

ARTICLE 328.

COSTS PAYABLE BY PERSONS CONVICTED OF TREASON OR FELONY.

[3] Any Court by which judgment is pronounced or recorded
upon the conviction of any person for treason or felony in
addition to such sentence as may otherwise by law be passed,

---

[1] 29 & 30 Vict. c. 52, s. 2.
[2] County, riding, division, city, or borough.
[3] 33 & 34 Vict. c. 23. s. 3.

may condemn such person to the payment of the whole or any part of the costs or expenses incurred in and about the prosecution and conviction for the offence of which he is convicted if to such Court it seems fit so to do. The payment of such costs or expenses, or any part thereof, may be ordered by the Court to be made out of any moneys taken from such person on his apprehension, or may be enforced at the instance of any person liable to pay, or who may have paid, the same in such and the same manner as the payment of any costs ordered to be paid by the judgment or order of any Court of competent jurisdiction in any civil action or proceeding may for the time being be enforced. In the meantime, and until the recovery of such costs and expenses from the person so convicted as aforesaid or from his estate, the same must be paid and provided for as if the Act for the Abolition of Forfeiture for Treason and Felony had not passed, and any money which may be recovered in respect thereof from the person so convicted or from his estate is applicable to the reimbursement of any person or fund by whom or out of which such costs and expenses have been paid or defrayed.

CHAPTER XXXVII.

REWARDS, COMPENSATION, AND RESTITUTION OF PROPERTY.

ARTICLE 329.

REWARDS AND COMPENSATION IN CERTAIN CASES.

[1] WHERE any person appears to any Court of oyer and terminer, gaol delivery, or [2] sessions of the peace, to have been active in or towards the apprehension of any person charged with any of the offences hereinafter mentioned, such Court may order the sheriff of the county in which the offence was committed to pay to the person who appears to the Court to have been active as aforesaid such sum or sums of money as to the Court seems reasonable and sufficient to compensate such person for his expenses, exertions, and loss of time in or towards such apprehension.

A sum ordered by a Court of quarter sessions to be paid to any one person in respect of any such offence except the offence of receiving stolen property, knowing the same to have been stolen, must not exceed £5.

The said offences are :—

Murder.

Feloniously and maliciously shooting at or attempting to discharge any kind of loaded fire-arms at any other person.

Stabbing.

Cutting.

Poisoning.

Administering anything to procure the miscarriage of any woman.

[1] 7 Geo. 4, c. 64, s. 28.
[2] 14 & 15 Vict. c. 55, s. 8.

Rape.

Burglary.

Housebreaking.

Robbery on the person.

Arson.

Horse-stealing.

Bullock-stealing.

Sheep-stealing.

Being accessory before the fact to any of the aforesaid offences.

Receiving stolen property knowing the same to have been stolen.

ARTICLE 330.

COMPENSATION TO FAMILY OF PERSON KILLED IN ARRESTING OFFENDERS.

[1] If any man happens to be killed in endeavouring to apprehend any person who is charged with any of the offences mentioned in Article 329, the Court before whom such person is tried may order the sheriff of the county to pay to the widow of the man so killed, in case he was married, or to his child or children, in case his wife is dead, or to his father or mother, in case he left neither wife nor child, such sum of money as to the Court, in its discretion, seems meet.

ARTICLE 331.

REWARDS AND COMPENSATION—HOW PAID.

[2] Every order for payment to any person in respect of the matters mentioned in Article 330, must be forthwith made out and delivered by the proper officer of the Court unto such person, [3] upon being paid for the same the sum of five shillings and no more, and the sheriff of the county for the time being must upon sight of such order forthwith pay

---

[1] 7 Geo. 4, c. 64, s. 30.

[2] Ibid. s. 29.

[3] The officer of a court of quarter sessions is not entitled to any fee, except when the offence charged is receiving stolen goods, and then he is entitled to a fee of five shillings.

to such person, or to any one duly authorized on his behalf, the money in such order mentioned.

Every such sheriff may immediately apply for repayment of the same to the Commissioners of the Treasury, who upon inspecting such order together with the acquittance of the person entitled to receive the money thereon, must forthwith order repayment to the sheriff of the money so by him paid.

ARTICLE 332.

COMPENSATION TO PERSONS INJURED BY FELONY.

[1] Any Court by which judgment is pronounced or recorded upon the conviction of any person for felony, may, if it thinks fit, upon the application of any person aggrieved, and immediately after such conviction, award any sum of money not exceeding £100 by way of satisfaction or compensation for any loss of property suffered by the applicant through or by means of the said felony.

The amount awarded for such satisfaction or compensation is deemed a judgment debt due to the person entitled to receive the same from the person so convicted. The order for payment of such amount may be enforced in the same manner as in the case of costs ordered by the Court to be paid under 33 & 34 Vict. c. 23, s. 3.[2]

ARTICLE 333.

RESTITUTION OF PROPERTY.

[3] Where any prisoner is convicted of larceny or other offence which includes the stealing of any property, and it appears to the Court by the evidence that the prisoner has sold the stolen property to any person, and that such person has had no knowledge that the same was stolen, and that any moneys have been taken from the prisoner on his apprehen-

---

[1] 33 & 34 Vict. c. 23, s. 4.
[2] See Article 321.
[3] 30 & 31 Vict. c. 35, s. 9.

sion, the Court may, on the application of such purchaser and on the restitution of the stolen property to the prosecutor, order that out of such moneys a sum not exceeding the amount of the proceeds of the said sale be delivered to the said purchaser.

INDEX.

LONDON: PRINTED BY WILLIAM CLOWES AND SONS, LIMITED, STAMFORD STREET
AND CHARING CROSS.

BY THE SAME AUTHOR.

A HISTORY OF THE CRIMINAL LAW OF ENGLAND. 3 vols. 8vo. 48s.

"This is the first time, we believe, though it is strange to have to say it, that the history of any great branch of English law, with the exception of purely Constitutional law, which belongs as much to historians as to lawyers, has been thoroughly worked out; and the task has been a formidable one, for almost everything had to be done from the beginning. . . . Mr. Justice Stephen has made it his business to track the true sources of the law through all the vast and miscellaneous mass of superincumbent comment and tradition. He has ransacked abridgments and reports of early cases, ill penned and worse printed, in a language made almost unintelligible by barbarisms and abbreviations. He has wrestled mightily with a host of perplexed statutes, of which not many lawyers know so much as the existence. The results of all this labour, a labour which can only be called enormous, are presented in an orderly and natural arrangement, and with an almost punctilious absence of technicality, so that not only are they intelligible to any reader of fair capacity and industry, but misunderstanding is hardly possible."—*The Times.*

A DIGEST OF THE CRIMINAL LAW: CRIMES AND PUNISHMENTS. New Edition. 8vo.
[*In the Press.*

"It occupies a position as a law text-book where it has no rivals. For the purpose of initiating the student—whether lawyer or layman—into the principles of the Criminal Law it would be impossible to find any more safe and sure plan than a careful study of this small book."—*The Times.*

A DIGEST OF THE LAW OF EVIDENCE. Fourth Edition. With New Preface. Crown 8vo. 6s.

"Students and practitioners will find no treatise on the law of evidence which is at the same time so systematic and so compendious. . . . No class will find greater advantage in the use of the digest than intelligent laymen, who, as justices or chairmen of Quarter Sessions, require an intelligible and trustworthy manual which is not rendered obscure by technical superfluities."—*Saturday Review.*

MACMILLAN AND CO., LONDON.

www.ingramcontent.com/pod-product-compliance
Lightning Source LLC
Chambersburg PA
CBHW030400270326
41926CB00009B/1204